The Little History of Lancashire

The Little History of Lancashire

Hugh Hollinghurst

First published 2024

The History Press
97 St George's Place, Cheltenham,
Gloucestershire, GL50 3QB
www.thehistorypress.co.uk

© Hugh Hollinghurst, 2024

The right of Hugh Hollinghurst to be identified as the
Author of this work has been asserted in accordance with
the Copyright, Designs and Patents Act 1988.

All rights reserved. No part of this book may be reprinted
or reproduced or utilised in any form or by any electronic,
mechanical or other means, now known or hereafter invented,
including photocopying and recording, or in any information
storage or retrieval system, without the permission in writing
from the Publishers.

British Library Cataloguing in Publication Data.
A catalogue record for this book is available from the British Library.

ISBN 978 1 80399 312 6

Typesetting and origination by The History Press.
Printed and bound in Great Britain by TJ Books Limited, Padstow, Cornwall.

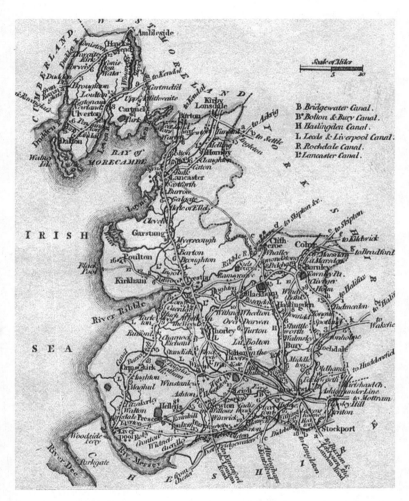

Map of Historic County of Lancashire in 1814 by John Cary in *Cary's Traveller's Companion*. Note the prominence given to roads, rivers and canals before the advent of railways.

CONTENTS

Acknowledgements   9

1   A Little Pre-History   11
2   The Romans Came, Saw, Conquered – and Went   17
3   Dark Ages and Light   27
4   Normans Herald the Medieval Age   37
5   Tudor Peace and Stuart War   51
6   Georgian Innovation and Change   69
7   The World's First Industrial Revolution   99
8   Victorian Philanthropy, Pleasure and Pain   145
9   Decline and Renewal   163

Bibliography   183
Index   187

ACKNOWLEDGEMENTS

Among the works listed in the bibliography, I have found the following particularly useful:

    Aspin, C., *Lancashire, The First Industrial Society*.
    Brazendale, David, *Lancashire's Historic Halls*.
    Crosby, Alan, *A History of Lancashire* .
    Gooderson, P.J., *A History of Lancashire*.
    Historical Society of Lancashire and Cheshire *Journals*.
    Wikimedia Commons for all the illustrations unless otherwise indicated.

Above all, I pay tribute to my wife Joan, without whose understanding and support this book could not have been written.

1

A LITTLE PRE-HISTORY

ADVENTURES OF AN ERRATIC BOULDER STONE

How was the landscape of the Historic County of Lancashire shaped? A boulder stone can tell you a story. Weighing in at 18 tons, it is a little sister of the 2,000-ton Bowder Stone in Borrowdale in the Lake District, created out of volcanic rock tens of millions years ago.

Comparatively recently, only a few thousand years ago, it was carried south during the glacial period over the sediments that had settled in the meantime. The earliest of these have bequeathed us the millstone grit and limestone of the Pennines. In the south-west of the county, later deposits were laid down of coal, marl and sandstone. The glacier carrying our 'erratic' boulder ground its way south over this terrain. As it journeyed, it spread a thick layer of clay over the Lancashire plain and river valleys. These give the distinctive pattern of a series of valleys that stretch down between the uplands of the Pennine hills in the east and the sea in the west.

Our boulder stone ended its journey at Crosby on the mouth of the River Mersey. There it rested until 1898 when workmen discovered it in a brickfield. With great labour and the help of a traction engine, it was transported from there to be the centrepiece of a road junction at the centre of the village. When that proved to be a hindrance to the flow of traffic, it was saved from destruction in the interests of science and placed in an honourable position in a nearby park, where it stands to this day.

The Bowder Stone in Borrowdale near Keswick in the Lake District. A plaque on the Boulder Stone in Crosby Coronation Park tells us that it consisted of gypsum (hydrous calcium sulphate) and its longitudinal axis was lying in a direction 48 degrees east of magnetic north.

After the boulder came to rest, when the glaciers were still retreating in about 10,000 BC, you can imagine hunter-gatherers chasing an elk, which is foraging with reindeer over the thinly vegetated tundra of the Fylde. They are armed with clubs and weapons tipped with 3in-long barbed bone points. The wounded animal escapes but falls, dying, into a muddy pool. In 1970 its skeleton, antlers and all, was discovered in a garden at Poulton-le-Fylde. During the interlude between this and the next scene the warming climate produces deciduous tree cover and vegetation more hospitable to people and animals.

Fossil Footprints and Aurochs

Picture a crowded Lancashire beach in prehistoric times. Wading birds abound and black and white oystercatchers with orange beaks and pink legs reap a rich harvest. Two huge cranes, larger than those we see today, are enacting a courting ritual. Huge aurochs (extinct wild cattle) dominate the scene. They dwarf the Stone Age men who are tracking red deer that have ventured out from the marshy, wooded hinterland and are roaming over the sands. Barefoot women are harvesting shrimps and razor-shellfish from a lagoon or gathering birds' eggs from the reeds that surround it. Children are playing in the sand and mud. Most are smaller in stature than us but probably have a healthy suntan, although some are hindered by physical difficulties: perhaps pregnancy, deformed feet or arthritis.

Not all of these scenes would be seen at the same period of time, but many have has been deduced or suggested by scientific observations made by Gordon Roberts of astonishing prints left on Formby Point.[1] The stage was set at the end of the last Ice Age. About 10,000 years ago sea levels rose and, in the melt down, a salt marsh was formed. Over the centuries, as sea levels stabilised and the tides retreated, a freshwater enclave of marsh and wood emerged that invited a variety of fauna and flora. Between 5000 and 2500 BC a thin stratum of sandy mud was formed, ready for imprints that were baked hard in the sun. Nowadays, before they are washed away by the sea, the footprints must be located and ideally photographed with measuring sticks for scientific research. This was achieved systematically from 1989 onwards. The latest research indicates that some of the semi-fossilised footprints may be 9,000 years old, dating to between 5350 and 3150 BC, that is, from the late Mesolithic to the mid-Neolithic Stone Age periods.

A complete red antler has been excavated from the later Stone Age period and hoofprints of domestic oxen have also been recorded. By analysing more than 200 human footprints, it has been calculated that the average heights for both male and female were smaller than ours today, although six-footers were not uncommon. Moccasin-like shoes have been observed but their bare feet show that they were troubled by many of the complaints we endure now: bunions, claw foot, high arch, bursitis and muscular dystrophy, not to say uncut toenails!

An awesome auroch, once widespread throughout Europe, including Formby and Martin Mere, but long extinct. (Courtesy W.G. Hale and Audrey Coney, *Martin Mere: Lancashire's Lost Lake*)

The most impressive tracks are those of the aurochs. The shoulder height of these fearsome beasts could measure 6ft and their length 11ft from muzzle to rump. With a hoofprint nearly a foot long, they had a stride of about 6–7ft and sported broad, elongated horns that could reach 31in long. However, although they could move swiftly, it appears they did so nervously and may not have been a danger unless provoked or attacked. Although depicted in Palaeolithic cave paintings 15,000 years ago and widespread throughout Europe, they finally became extinct in Poland in 1627. Formby has the best-preserved remains of its tracks.

Massive auroch hoofprints – twice the size of cattle prints – have also been discovered in the silt of Martin Mere. Prints of wolves, the antlers of red deer and the bones of boar and sheep show that they also once roamed the area. An elk with antlers 'two yards across' was found buried below the peat. Geese, ducks and wildfowl have bred here since before the nineteenth century, most notably mallard, teal, shoveler and possibly tufted duck. The black-headed gull may have nested on islands in the mere and local people still take eggs for food in the spring.

CELTIC VIEWS, AXES AND SKULLS

Near the village of Bleasdale, high in the nearby fells, are the remains of a wooden henge circle dating from the early Bronze Age, maybe about 2,000 BC. Concrete posts mark the place where the wooden timbers originally stood before they were removed to Preston Museum for preservation. Gradually, from about this time, the Celts arrived. From hunting and gathering, they turned to converting the deciduous forest to farmland using flint axes and other tools.

Stone circles, hill forts and cairns indicate aesthetic appreciation, a religious outlook or territorial awareness, as in the cluster of sites in the Ulverston area. Here, commanding a beautiful view across the Leven Estuary and Morecambe Bay, a circle of stones at Sunbrick is surrounded by bracken on Birkrigg Common. A younger hillfort nearby at Skelmore Heads, Urswick, known locally as the Druid's Circle, utilises the edge of a limestone scar to span the southern half of the Furness peninsula with two stone concentric circles bearing signs of ceremonial activity. Remains of five cremations have been discovered, one with an inverted urn.

The Iron Age came in gradually between 800 and 500 BC. With this more settled way of life, communities could build monuments and afford to trade as well. As can be seen from the illustration on page 16, socketed axes from this period are well preserved and beautifully decorated.

Looking down the valley towards Whalley at Portfield, excavations have revealed life in Iron Age times but there were almost certainly settlements on the site going back to 4,000 BC. Finds that bear witness to the civilised people who lived there include axes, a sharp, pointed knife, stud, gauge and part of a hilt.

Of particular interest, all from the Bronze Age, are a penannular brooch (a loop of metal with an attached moveable pin), possibly of Irish craftmanship, a gold tress-ring (for binding the hair) and a biconical vessel (in the form of two cones joined point to point).

In contrast, finds have been made in the bogs and marshes of lower-lying land. Indeed, during excavation work associated with Preston Dock in 1885, a sensational discovery unearthed thirty human skulls, sixty pairs of red deer antlers, forty-three ox skulls, two pilot whale skulls and two dugout canoes. Recent research has revealed traces of trackways, grazing land and permanent settlements. These consisted of circular huts roofed with branches and then covered by skins or thatch. Each of them was probably inhabited by an extended family.

By the time the Romans arrived to usher in the next scene, the local tribes seem to have come under the aegis of the Brigantes, a tribe whose influence spread from a centre in Yorkshire over the north-west from coast to coast.

Iron Age axe heads from Skelmore Heads with beautiful decorations.

2

THE ROMANS CAME, SAW, CONQUERED – AND WENT

VENI VIDI VICI (JULIUS CAESAR), 'I CAME, I SAW, I CONQUERED' – BUT NOT HERE IN LANCASHIRE

Julius Caesar made two reconnaissance expeditions in 55 and 54 BC and temporarily occupied part of south-east England. This was followed up a century later by an invasion under the Emperor Claudius and Roman civilisation then spread to the north-west. There are no Roman villas in Lancashire that are confirmed by archaeology (but many, for example, in Yorkshire and only one in Cheshire). It seems that Roman civilisation here was largely confined to forts and their accompanying '*vici*' (not 'I conquered' in this context, but villages that grew up outside the forts to provide services for those inside). They made little impact on the settled way of life that Celtic farmers and communities led in Lancashire. Finally, in AD 383, after three centuries of occupation, the Romans withdrew their forces from Britain starting in the north and west of the island.

'BEFORE THE ROMAN CAME TO RYE ...

... the rolling English drunkard made the rolling English road' (G.K. Chesterton, 'The Rolling English Road', 1913). But the Romans planned their straight and direct network carefully, constructed by the army primarily for military reasons. The line of the route was surveyed; there were no problems of land ownership to be overcome; and construction was immediate, well maintained and lasting. One of them led over the Pennines from Manchester to York. Remarkable remains can be observed at Blackstone Edge near Littleborough where a paved road with a central gutter runs through a sunken stretch of land (a holloway). Although suggested to be a turnpike road, it is overlaid with medieval features in places and only the Romans could have constructed a road of that quality before then. The best view of a typical straight line of a Roman road, maybe even in England, can be viewed from Jeffrey Hill above Longridge. Look north along the line of the road from Ribchester to a fort at Burrow in Lonsdale, 2 miles south of Kirby Lonsdale. The summit of Pen-y-Ghent, the sighting point for the Roman surveyors, can also be seen in the far distance.

A Queen, Faithful to the Romans, Unfaithful to her Husband

From their initial landings in the south-east, roads were crucial in the Roman advance to the north-west. The road network linked up with forts at Chester and York, which were established in the AD 70s. The Romans were then in a position to advance into the territory of the Brigantes, a tribe covering the north of England. Here, Queen Cartimandua and her husband Vinutius befriended the Romans and suppressed an anti-Roman faction. Then, when Caratacus, the national leader of the opponents of Rome, was defeated in battle and fled to her for protection she promptly reinforced her loyalty by handing him over to the invaders. When Vinutius became alienated from his wife, she seized his brother and other relatives. He retaliated by invading her kingdom but Cartimandua was reinstated by the Romans. She scandalously replaced Vinutius with his armour bearer, but the infuriated Vinutius returned to the fray and again she had to be rescued by the Romans. The quarrel was ended when a new Roman governor, Agricola, took control. His biography, written by the Roman historian Tacitus, is the best historical record for this period of Britain.

The Romans Invent our Motorway Network

The network of Roman roads in the region was constructed by the army for the military purposes of supply and policing, as in the rest of the province. The first one to be constructed in Lancashire may have been from Chester.

M6: The road from the south crossed the River Mersey at its first fordable point at Wilderspool (near the Thelwall Viaduct) where there was a Roman *'mansio'*, or lodge, for travellers. It grew into a small industrial town manufacturing bronze, iron, glass and pottery.

M62: There seems to have been a road from Wilderspool to Manchester (Roman Mamucium), from which radiated at least three Roman roads. One led over the hills to York. Alongside it, at Blackstone Edge near Littleborough, stands a mysterious grit stone pillar called the Aiggin, which is possibly a waymarker for the pack horse route, also marking the boundary between Lancashire and Yorkshire. Originally 7ft high, it has fallen or been pushed over and reduced to 4ft. It is incised with a Latin cross and the enigmatic letters I and T, possibly standing for the Latin I(n) T(e) 'In you' (we trust). The name is said to be derived from the French *aiguille* (needle) or *aigle* (eagle). It shows how the road enjoyed a continuity of use from Roman times through centuries to the later period.

M61: Another Roman road radiating from Manchester led towards the River Ribble. On the way, you pass another early medieval cross at Affetside, once again showing a continuity of use. At the Ribble, a bridge was protected by a fort at Ribchester which, like Manchester, was a hub for radiating Roman roads.

M55: Want to visit Blackpool? Take the Roman road from Ribchester travelling west and well marked on the Ordnance Survey map. This would take you through what is now Preston to Kirkham, where there was a small fort, probably to maintain a cavalry presence.

M6: If you wanted to go north or south from Ribchester, you would travel on the Roman equivalent of the M6. This continued north from Wilderspool on the Mersey crossing to Lancaster, passing through Wigan (Roman Coccium), where there was probably a fort, to Walton-le-Dale near Preston. There, a Roman military supply depot has been unearthed with finds of silver, lead, pottery, wine, oil, glass and jewellery. Nearly every site in Roman Britain reveals Samian ware. Made out of red clay, it made a long journey by sea and road from the centre of France where it had been designed and manufactured. One example unearthed at Walton-le-Dale was richly decorated with a centaur, sea bull, panther and Mercury. The Roman road bypassed Preston, thus anticipating the construction in 1958 of the first motorway in Britain, the Preston bypass! The road proceeds onwards to Lancaster (called Galacum by the Romans). Here it travels north towards Hadrian's Wall. There, many mortaria (kitchen vessels) have been found that were manufactured at Wilderspool, where our journey started. Like our motorways, Roman roads stimulated trade and prosperity.

-CHESTER/-CASTER/-CESTER

Place names ending in -chester/-caster/-cester/-ceister proclaim the site of a Roman fort. These endings are derived from the Latin word *castra*, meaning a camp. The first part of the name may be an adaptation of the Roman word of the fortification or a local place. Ribchester was therefore the site of a Roman fort on the banks of the River Ribble. Its Roman name was Bremetennacum Veteranorum (of the veterans) and indicates that it was eventually garrisoned by veteran soldiers. At first, soldiers were recruited from Spain and Hungary in accordance with the common Roman practice of using foreign, not local, troops to garrison their provinces. It may be that when the Hungarians retired, their home territory had been abandoned by the Romans in the meantime and they could not be returned to their homeland. They were therefore retained at Ribchester, which was accorded special status and importance and became a centre of the region.

Underfloor Air Ventilation

The fort housed a cavalry unit to maintain order and protect the Roman settlements. It was originally built in the AD 70s with a rampart of turf topped by a wooden palisade. Timber barracks were built and stables were constructed with timber stakes driven into the ground, walls made from wattle and daub, and straw floor coverings. The fortifications were extended and later replaced in stone along with the gatehouses, towers and main buildings to combat threats and uncertainties associated with the local tribe of the Brigantes. A stone slab records that the construction was carried out by a legion based in Chester, the 'XX Valeria Victrix' (Twentieth Victorious Valerian), probably in honour of a victory obtained under their commander Valerius. The fort was constructed in a Roman standard design for infantry and adapted for cavalry occupation. It contained three most important central elements: granaries with underfloor air ventilation, the commander's house and a headquarters building where all the troops could assemble and be given their orders. Four stone columns from one of the buildings adorn the entrance to the White Bull pub in the village and there are mysterious Roman Tuscan columns in the church that may have come from the fort.

Come Out of the Fort and Enjoy Yourself in our Village

Outside a fort a *vicus* (village) grew up that would develop into a thriving community of its own with links to the outside world.

You can imagine how they might advertise their attractions:

Do you want new armour and weapons? Our metal and leather workers will supply them.

Does your equipment need repairing? Our joinery shops offer excellent service.

Do you dream of shaking off the strict military discipline in the fort? Drink, gamble and socialise with us!

Are you tired of a standard military meat diet? Supplement it at our butchers with extra beef, mutton, pork, goatmeat, venison, fowl and fish.

Our bathhouse provides all the facilities a Roman soldier deserves: a changing room, cold plunge pool and three rooms heated by a furnace. Enjoy a hot water bath, a steamy sauna or a chat in a warm relaxing atmosphere.

Our women are excellent company. Form a long-term relationship. Think of marriage and a happy family life.

See the tombstone of Julius Maximus, a soldier in the guard of the governor. The inscription affectionately records the death of his wife, who lived 38 years, 2 months and 8 days; their son, who lived 6 years, 3 months and 20 days; and her mother, who lived until she was 50. Julius set up the memorial to his 'incomparable' wife; his son, who was 'most devoted' to his father; and to his 'most steadfast' mother-in-law.

Exciting Discoveries

The whole complex of fort and *vicus* was surrounded by a Punic ditch (an extra line of defence that was dug in a V shape with one

The Ribchester Helmet, now on display at the British Museum, dates from the late first or early second century. It was found by a clog maker, bought by antiquarian Charles Townley of Towneley Hall and on his death sold to the museum by his heir and cousin.

side much steeper than the other). Two particularly interesting objects have been excavated. The gravestone of a spirited horse and horseman was found in the River Ribble in 1876. He was inscribed as coming from Asturias in Spain. Shown bareheaded with a luxurious crop of hair, he is spearing an adversary underfoot. A ceremonial helmet (pictured above), one of the finest items of bronze work ever found in Britain, was discovered by a boy in 1796. The skull part of the helmet is decorated with a battle scene of eleven combatants on foot and, significantly, six on horseback. Originally gilded or silvered, the helmet would have been worn by a skilled rider in a show where the cavalry practised and demonstrated their skills. It was purchased by antiquarian collector Charles Townley of nearby Towneley Hall and then sold on to the British Museum but a replica is displayed in Ribchester Museum.

A Signalling System

A Roman signal station used to stand on Mellor Moor, 2 miles to the south of a fort. It was situated strategically, so that signals could be sent by fire or smoke between there and a fort on Carr Hill, Kirkham, nearer to the Ribble Estuary and the sea. Its outline is difficult to decipher now because of overploughing, two excavations and overgrowing vegetation but it consisted of a wooden tower surrounded by a ditch and bank and possibly a slight timber palisade. It was probably part of a wider system that linked up with Burrow in Lonsdale in the north and possibly west, where there are good views. However, to get past Whalley and beyond Pendle, a further three stations would be needed to obtain good sightings.

A Christian Acrostic

Mamucium was a Roman fort with a hill shaped liked a breast (Latin *mamma*), hence Manchester. A fragment of stone was discovered there dated to the second century AD. On it was inscribed a Latin acrostic, which could be evidence of Christianity, as shown in the following table.

Usually in an acrostic the initial letters of a series of words form another word. In this case, the initial letters do so reading across, down and in reverse, and can be translated accordingly as well ('the sower Arepo directs the wheels in his work'). If each letter is removed and displayed in the shape of a cross, it forms the Latin for 'Our Father' horizontally and vertically. There are two As and two Os left over as shown, which could represent the Greek letters Alpha and Omega, the first and last letters of the Greek alphabet, symbolising the eternity of God. It might therefore be interpreted as a secret Christian sign.

ROTAS	WHEELS	P
OPERA	WORK	A
TENET	HOLDS	A T Ω
AREPO	AREPO	E
SATOR	SOWER	R
	That is:	PATERNOSTER
	Arepo	O
	the sower	S
	directs	A T Ω
	the wheels	E
	in his work	R

Threats from the Sea

Two altars have been found at Lancaster Roman fort (Galacum). One is dedicated to Mars, the Roman god of war. That is nothing unusual as Mars was one of the twelve Olympians who formed the pantheon of the Greek and Roman gods. What is unusual is that the altar was dedicated not just by the Commander Sabinus but also by the company of bargemen who were under his control. There was a series of forts built on the site, culminating in a coastal defence fortification that was also a supply base built in the fourth century AD. This was to combat the threat coming from the sea, not just from Ireland but from the Saxons. It formed part of a coastal defence line along the west of Britain.

Caught in an Ambush?

At Ribchester, another altar is unusual because it is dedicated to an extremely rare god, Lalonus Contrebis, maybe a god of the meadowland, who is described as *sanctissimus* (very holy). Only two other altars have been discovered with his name, one in Yorkshire and the other in Provence, where the god is allied to Fortuna (good luck). This is near to Spain, where there was a centre called Contrebia and troops from Spain were stationed in Ribchester. Julius Januarius, the dedicator of the altar, announces himself as a former *decurion* (an officer commanding a troop of about thirty cavalrymen) who was *emeritus* (retired, like present-day professors). He says he set up the altar to fulfil a vow. Can we imagine he was caught in the meadowlands, surrounded by a rebellious tribe and, despairing of his life, prayed to his ancestral god, who by good luck saved him?

3

DARK AGES AND LIGHT

ANGLO-SAXONS INVADE

During the Roman occupation of Britain, the life of most of the Celtic population continued as before. When Rome was captured by the Goths in AD 410, the Roman garrisons were withdrawn from Britain. Use of Latin in social life and in the army ended, organised maintenance of the roads ceased and the forts were adapted for other purposes or robbed for use as building material. North-west England truly entered a dark age. The civilising influence of the Romans and historic evidence both disappear from view.

It seems that the Romans may have adopted a scorched earth policy when they abandoned Ribchester. The only standing structures are those of the granaries, and they bear scorch marks as if they had been deliberately razed to avoid the enemy using them to their advantage later. The forts would have crumbled anyway through lack of maintenance and been taken over by British Celts. They lived in the buildings or adapted them for other uses, or they incorporated the materials in other structures. These can give valuable evidence of the Roman occupation. Ribchester church is built within the confines of the Roman fort, for example, and whole columns from the fort seem to have been embodied in the church. Innumerable individual and unidentified bricks and stones scattered in medieval buildings will have a story to tell of Roman times.

Even before the Romans left Britain in the fifth century, Anglo-Saxons had raided Britain. After that, their penetration into England was slow, starting in the south-east. DNA analysis suggests that there is minor Anglo-Saxon influence on the gene pool of the south-east of England, let alone the north-west. Their advance into the north-west may have been from over the Pennines. Place names can indicate where Anglo-Saxons settled. For example, the -ton suffix comes from the Old English for a farm or estate and there are more than 200 examples of this in Lancashire. Eccles is especially interesting. It is derived from the Greek for an assembly or church (hence ecclesiastical) and appears both by itself and with the addition of -ton. This is a sign of the spread of Christianity that was reignited in England by the arrival of St Augustine of Canterbury in 597.

From Kings Down to Slaves

A hierarchy of rule and service stratified during the Anglo-Saxon period. The king was the main landholder but an aristocracy of earls also held large tracts of land. Subservient to them were thegns (thanes), who were lords of the manors, and drengs. Both classes owed service to the king, especially for supplying soldiers in times of war. Burgesses were townsmen, whose tenure was based on a financial payment. Radmen (riding men) performed errands for the king. All these were free men. Below them was a large class of villeins, small landowners owing services to the lord of the manor. 'Borders' owned less land than villeins and may have been ex-slaves, and oxmen may have had ploughing duties. At the bottom of the pile were the slaves with very little freedom. They worked for their masters but might have a little property and saved up for their freedom by working in their spare time.

Living conditions for the villagers were primitive. Their cottages, which they built themselves out of mud and wood, were so low they could scarcely stand upright. The roofs were covered with timber or thatch and the earth floor was strewn with rushes.

They were kept warm by a fire in the middle and by the livestock that surrounded them (excellent environmentally, but what a hard life!). Porridge and vegetables were cooked on the fire, but oatmeal bread and beer would have to be brought in. Ewes and cows provided milk. If it could be afforded, salt was obtained from Furness or Cheshire to cure meat for the winter.

VIKINGS, DANES OR NORSEMEN?

What do we call the people who raided Britain from the tenth century onwards, were a threat to the unity of the country and contributed one of her most famous kings? King Cnut was a Dane (also King of Norway) and the Dane Law controlled the north of England for more than a century. But the invaders of the north-west came from Norway not Denmark, and were Norwegians or Norsemen. So, they were ancestors of the Norman invaders to come! It is perhaps better to call them Vikings, a generic term for Scandinavian adventurers. Their impact on the north-west can be gauged from the large number of place names ending in, for example, -by (*bei* is the Viking name for a village) compared with other parts of the country. Viking ancestors might also be found in places ending -dale and -irk, Scandinavian for valley and church. The same evidence points to an invasion route possibly via Yorkshire or a retreat that way, but more probably via Ireland and the Isle of Man.

The Vikings would progress from raiders to traders to peaceful settlers. Eventually they integrated with the inhabitants, in spite of the difficulty of religious reconciliation between the Hammer and the Cross. A peaceful settlement might be achieved by the Vikings taking over low-lying marsh and boggy terrain or other land that the earlier Anglo-Saxons had rejected as unsuitable for cultivating. Thingwall near West Derby (and also on the Wirral) is particularly significant. Its counterpart in the Isle of Man is Tynewald, the site of the Thing, a form of government brought over by the Vikings that was conducted through assizes.

Celtic Crosses

A Celtic cross (now in the British Museum) was found buried in the churchyard of Lancaster Priory (St Mary's parish Church). The site dates back to Roman times (AD 200) but became a Christian enclave in the seventh century and the cross probably dates from the ninth or early tenth century. Cuthbertson, named in the inscription, may have been a king or prince of Northumbria. The kingdom of Northumbria intermittently covered parts of Lancashire as far south as the Mersey from the seventh century until the Norman conquest. A battle was fought at Whalley in AD 798 to decide which regional potentate would control the area.

There are delightful panels on a Celtic cross in the graveyard of Halton-on-Lune Church near Lancaster that illustrate scenes from the Viking story of Sigurd the dragon slayer. They are the most complete telling of the saga outside Scandinavia.

In St Oswald's Church in Winwick, a cross bears the gruesome image of a saint, probably Oswald, being martyred. Two soldiers are hanging the saint upside down from a tree, each having a foot on his face.

There are no fewer than three mysterious Celtic crosses in Whalley church yard, which were reinstated by the vicar after being thrown down during the Commonwealth.

Recreation of a Celtic cross found at Lancaster inviting you to pray for Cynebalth Cuthbertson. It is written in the runic alphabet, which originated in Scandinavia. (Reproduced with the kind permission of the editor and council of the Historic Society of Lancashire and Cheshire *Transactions*, Vol. 45, J. Romilly Allen)

Cockle Shells or Silver Coins?

At 6 p.m. on 15 May 1840, workmen were repairing the banks of the River Ribble at Cuerdale near Preston. They spotted a chest lying in a rift in the earth where insistent rain had caused a landslide into the river. One of the workmen burst the chest open, exclaiming how 'quare' it was to find cockle shells there. But there was a tradition of buried treasure along this stretch of the Ribble and they had actually discovered 8,600 items of bullion, mostly silver, the biggest such anywhere outside Russia. Out of the near 8,000 coins, each worker received just one. The rest were declared treasure trove and are now part of the collection of the British Museum.

The discovery of any hoard immediately provokes mysteries. Why was it buried and who did it? Celtic and Anglo-Saxon peoples might hoard for religious purposes in the afterlife, or as a display of wealth and power or to stow valuables for safety in troubled times. However, the amount of coin, jumble of bullion and lack of intact jewellery point to a war chest. The dates of the coins confirm this. The Anglo-Saxon coins are chiefly of Alfred the Great, Edward the Elder and Edmund, but the latest coins are those of Louis the Blind, Emperor of the West Franks in AD 901–905. This gives the approximate date of the hoard, which could have been for the payment of soldiers. At that time, the Vikings had been ejected from Ireland and may have been preparing to cross the Irish Sea to reoccupy Dublin. There is a significant amount of Irish jewellery in the hoard. The Vikings ruled the north of England under the Dane Law agreement between them and Alfred the Great.

Most of the coins were from the Dane Law region but there were about a thousand each of Anglo-Saxon and Frankish origin and a handful from Scandinavia, the Islamic world and eastern Europe. The rarest one had had a long journey in space and time, from Byzantium and dated AD 615–30. Some of the bullion had been melted down into ingots or chopped up ready for the melting pot or to be given in payment. Brooches and arm rings in fragments were amongst loot from Ireland and neck rings came from Scandinavia. The whole reflects trade or raiding links centred in York and Dublin that would have brought wealth into the area about AD 905–10, and is of European significance. The tradition that 'by standing on the bridge at Walton-le-Dale and looking towards Ribchester one could gaze over the richest treasure in England' may have been enshrined in local folklore for centuries and argues for a continuity of settlement.

BURIED, FOUND AND LOST

Sometime during the troubles of the early tenth century, an Anglo-Saxon could be seen digging frantically in woodland on a knoll rising above marshland. He was burying his treasure before fleeing from the Vikings and never returned to claim it. Six centuries later, in the religious turmoil at the start of the reign of James I, William Blundell, Catholic recusant and Lord of the Manor of Little Crosby, decided to create a secret Catholic graveyard (called Harkirk) in the woods near his estate at Little Crosby (the -by shows it was a village of Viking origin). On 8 April 1611, the day after the first burial in the graveyard, William Blundell recorded that a servant boy named Thomas, 'dryvinge my Catle (which as yett did nightlie lye in the howse) to a field neare the sayde place of buriall', found some ancient coins that had been buried but were disturbed by the digging. On investigation, further coins were found, to a total of over eighty. William and his household had never seen anything like them, 'none bigger than a groate, and none less than a twoe pence'. (William's spelling is unusually idiosyncratic). He set to work to delve into the origins of the coins, with the help of books in his library. His reading was wide and he was unusually well acquainted with some of the major authors of the past. William carefully copied thirty-five of them in pen and ink and had an engraving made on a copper plate (illustrated). Prints were made from this, eventually up to 200, which 'flew abroad in ye country'.

These coins he kept in his possession, though they were subsequently lost during the Civil War. William Blundell the Cavalier had sent them with other valuables to his relations in Wrexham, ironically, 'for better security in ye tyme of war'. The remainder were melted down and turned into a chalice and a pyx.

Nationally, the Harkirk Hoard was the first discovery of buried coins of the Anglo-Saxon period and was therefore, and has remained, of the greatest interest to antiquarians and numismatists. There must be many more hoards waiting to be unearthed. Here's hoping!

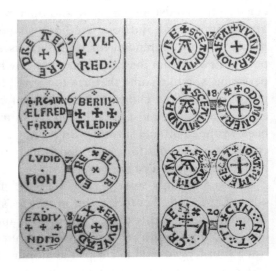

The Harkirk Hoard was deposited just before the Anglo-Saxons, faced with Viking attacks in AD 910, retreated to Northumbria. Numismatists have identified in it the coinage of kings: Alfred the Great, Edward the Elder and Cnut of Northumbria (not the later, more famous, King of England). (Courtesy Mark Blundell Prints)

St Patrick and a Hogback

St Patrick was born in fifth-century England but was captured by pirates and spent six years in Ireland. He then made a dramatic escape to return home. Local tradition claims he was shipwrecked at Heysham, and St Patrick's Chapel, overlooking Morecambe Bay, was founded by the saint himself. It is true that it would be natural to land there after crossing the Irish Sea (as travellers do on the ferry service!) but there is no corroborative evidence that it was at this particular point. After training as a missionary on the Continent, St Patrick returned to Ireland to convert the island to Christianity and missionaries from there subsequently converted England to the faith. Although excavations have revealed traces of an even earlier chapel, the ruin that bears the saint's name nevertheless dates from the eighth or ninth century, which makes it the oldest surviving religious building in the county. An Anglo-Saxon doorway that looks out from the rocky headland is arched with a stone lintel in a decorative curved pattern.

Close by the remains of the chapel are six pre-Conquest graves cut into the sandstone, on view and open to the elements. Two are straight sided and four are body shaped. All have socket holes, probably intended for timber crosses. Their prominent position away from the chapel may indicate burials of important personages, while some that are too small for full-sized adults may have interred children. The adjacent cemetery contained eighty burials, the most notable being a woman thought to have been wrapped up in a shroud with an Anglo-Scandinavian bone comb. It is unusual for grave goods to be part of a Christian burial, but not for a pagan one.

Only a few yards away, a rare 'hogback' monument, the only one in Lancashire, lies recumbent in St Peter's Church, Heysham. Two metres long, it is carved out of red sandstone and shaped like a Viking longhouse dating from about 920–950. At each end a four-legged animal clasps the monument in its paws. The carvings on each side could represent part of the Viking Sigmund legend or contain Christian symbolism. In a society where both Christians and pagans lived together it is difficult to tell which, or it could be both. To a pagan, Christianity meant the adoption of a Christian god to run alongside their own but for a Christian it meant complete renunciation of the pagan gods.

Carved on this side of the Heysham Hogback are five wolves (or hounds), four men and a hart on the main panel. Above, two wolves (or hounds) accompany a man lying prone. On the other side, a man beside a great tree is surrounded by animals.

4

NORMANS HERALD THE MEDIEVAL AGE

His Mother Led a Colourful and Wicked Life

When Duke William conquered England in 1066, he granted most of the lands of the English nobility to his followers. One of the most loyal and trusted, Roger de Poitou, was granted the 'land between the Ribble and the Mersey' together with parts of what later became Cumberland and Westmorland[2]. His father was Roger de Montgomery, who held estates in Normandy, was a councillor for William in his invasion and after the Battle of Hastings became the greatest landholder in England. His mother was a French noblewoman, Mabel de Bellême, who inherited vast estates in Normandy and was described as 'small in stature, talkative, clever, and witty'.[3] She led a colourful but wicked life. In a family feud, she poisoned the heir to an estate to secure it for herself and deprived many more landlords of their land. In a final feud, she was decapitated by her rival when coming out of her bath. Robert, her eldest son, inherited her vast landholdings and also her cruelty but Roger de Poitou seems to have been untainted. He strengthened his hold on the region by constructing a castle as his headquarters at Lancaster on the site of the Roman fort. The only castle in South Lancashire then existing was at Penwortham. He himself cannot have seen much of his distant Lancashire domain, although it formed the largest part of his estates: eight of them stretched down as far as Hampshire. Besides possible time-consuming visits to these, he campaigned in France for Rufus, William's successor, but rebelled unsuccessfully against Henry I. His lands passed to Robert and he retired to his wife's holdings in Poitou in France.

Exempt from Paying Dues for Highway Robbery

Following the Norman Conquest, large holdings were left in the hands of Anglo-Saxons. One of these was Uhtred, who was lord of fifteen manors that stretched from Einulvesdel (Ainsdale) in the north to Spec (Speke) in the south. Besides these, he also held manors in Cheshire. We are told[4] that in Crosby and Kirkdale he was exempt from all customary dues, except for some breaches of the peace: highway robbery (!); breaking and entry; a combat that persisted after an oath was taken; if a man did not pay what he owed after the judgement of a Reeve (an Anglo-Saxon district official) or did not heed a boundary set by the Reeve. But he did pay the king's tax like everyone else in the district. We wish we knew more about Uhtred and his ancestry.

Domesday

Twenty years after his conquest, William sent commissioners all over the country to find out how much each landholder held in land and livestock and what it was worth. His grandson, Bishop Henry of Winchester, said that its purpose was that every man 'should know his right and not usurp another's' and 'the natives called it the Domesday Book, by analogy from the Day of Judgment'[5] because it was the final authoritative register of rightful possession. It covers the old English society, which although under new management had not changed.

Most of the population lived in villages. Their houses might be clustered together or dispersed among the fields. They had their say in local assemblies, albeit dominated by the lords of the manors whose holdings would vary from tiny homesteads to vast estates. The region was covered with woodland in the hilly country to the east and north, mosses and peat to the west, and arable land in between, largely cleared of woodland. 'Earl Harold' (William did not recognise him as king) is only mentioned twice. He held outliers – land that was separated from the main body of a manor.

Hundreds

The Domesday Book tells us in amazing detail about the state of individual manors with a huge variation in size. In Lancashire, they were grouped into six districts called 'hundreds'. These were assemblies of notables and village representatives who met about once a month for administration, so called maybe because in general they could afford to provide the monarch with 100 men in war. They were composed of manors. The smallest of these were valued at 32d (old pence) with only about 120 acres. The largest was (West) Derby with about twelve times as much. Eight men held the manor between them with four ploughs belonging to the lord. There were forty-six villagers and sixty-two smallholders with twenty-three ploughs between them. There were also two male and three female 'slaves' (a relic of Anglo-Saxon practice). The woodland was about 5 miles long and 2½ miles wide with three hawk's eyries. These were often recorded in the book along with 'hays' or enclosures for trapping deer. Rivers provided fish. Pigs were reared on acorns from neighbouring woodland. But the frequent references to ploughs indicate that crops grown on arable land were the most common source of sustenance. Although Saxon material has been excavated on the site of a church at West Derby, there was no mention of a priest. Priests' churches at Walton and Childwall served the area. There were only one or two churches at the most in each hundred and it seems that initially, under the Normans, Christianity had regressed.

Wasteland

The Normans took over the social scale of the Anglo-Saxons but the standard of living deteriorated. The value of each hundred had decreased since the time of King Edward the Confessor. South of the Ribble, many manors had been held by Edward and then briefly by Harold II in 1066 although, naturally, this was not recognised in the Domesday Book. Similarly, north of the Ribble, many manors had been held by Earl Tostig, Harold's brother. He allied himself with the Norwegian king, who claimed the throne along with William and Harold. Both of them were killed at the Battle of Stamford Bridge before William's victory over Harold at the Battle of Hastings.

We know that there was a rebellion soon after William took over the throne and he 'harried' the north with great cruelty and destruction. It seems that this was most severe in 'Yorkshire', where out of about sixty unidentified manors only sixteen 'had a few inhabitants ... the rest are waste'.[6] Some of these may be Lancastrian as the region (Amounderness) was based on Preston. One manor in Lancashire (Leyland) is described in this way as being 'partly waste', although this could be for other reasons. So the region may have escaped the worst.

There was no sign of any town. Although Penwortham boasted four burgesses, that is hardly a town. They were probably in the service of Roger de Poitou's castle there, but this was replaced by his castle at Lancaster, which became the county town.

Sexual Discrimination

Some landholders held more than one manor. The manors varied in the laws they enforced and the punishments they inflicted. In general, these were more severe in Lancashire than Cheshire and indicate that life north of the Mersey was wilder and less civilised. Between the Ribble and Mersey, the fine for violence against women was only one quarter of the fine for the same offence in Cheshire and was less than the fine imposed on a representative who wilfully absented himself from a shire court meeting. There, certain offenders paid a double fine if an offence was committed on a Sunday or during a holy season. But in the wilder district north of the Mersey, all days were esteemed alike.

Motte and Bailey

One of the Normans' first and highest priorities was to secure their military position by the construction of castles. Although the primary purpose of a castle was military, to be used as a base of operations and to control the surrounding areas, it also stood as a stamp of authority over the population of an area and a status symbol. The earliest castles were built of wood in strategic lowland areas such as Lancaster, Tulketh (Preston), Penwortham and Warrington. Later these would be converted into stone, and others constructed in remote areas where they would dominate an upland scene, as at Clitheroe. Here, a possible date is 1186–87, when a chapel was dedicated to St Michael on the same site and confirmed by the Pope. His protection of the chapel was guaranteed by giving him the right to tithes from the land of Robert de Lacey and others, which included mills, fishponds, foals, calves, cheese, butter, hunting and animals in the forests. A century later, when Whalley Abbey was founded, a descendant (also Robert de Lacy) swapped back the abbey and its church for Clitheroe Castle Chapel and the right of hunting in the forests! As shown today by a climb up to the remains of the castle, Robert also gained a valuable safeguard against quarrels between local families of the time. It affords a panoramic view of the surrounding countryside that would have enabled the approach of hostile forces to be seen well in advance.

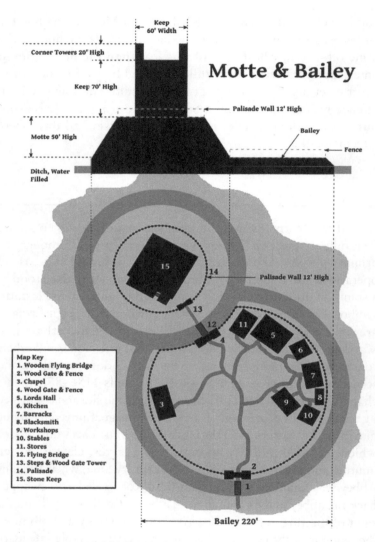

A Norman motte-and-bailey castle: a keep maybe 70ft high on raised ground (motte, maybe 50ft high) could only be approached by a courtyard (bailey) protected by a palisade and ditch. The bailey could encompass (clockwise from one o'clock) stores, lord's hall, kitchen, barracks, smithy, workshops, stables and (separated) chapel.

The Botelers ('butlers') of Warrington were rivals, and like the de Lacys rarely attended their Lancashire estates because of their far-flung holdings elsewhere that demanded their services to the king. Warrington Castle was one of the largest motte-and-bailey castles in the Historic County of Lancashire (now in Cheshire). William Boteler contributed 200 archers to the campaigns of Edward I in Wales and Scotland. In return, he received a charter for his growing township in Warrington (a Boteler school remains there to this day).

Strict Cistercians

With the Normans began a great surge in founding abbeys. This was part of their policy of imposing their authority through religion and impressive buildings. Many churches and castles were also constructed. Furness Abbey was the second richest in the kingdom (after Fountains in Yorkshire). It had a noble founder, Count Stephen of Blois in Normandy (grandson of William the Conqueror and, later, King Stephen). In 1124 he founded a monastery of reformative monks from Savigny in Normandy at Tulketh near Preston. In their turn, they founded another daughter house at Furness. The site was chosen, as often by a community of monks, for the availability of water, productive land, and building material such as stone and timber. It was remote, which ensured the purity of the order, but offered easy communication by sea across Morecambe Bay and beyond. Although this could be perilous, it was quicker and less arduous than the journey by land.

In 1147 the Savignac order was taken over by the Cistercians. They followed a strict, simple and austere rule of life in diet, clothing and personal wealth with manual labour in the fields. This was founded on a cycle of worship and prayer at regular three-hour intervals night and day, which the monks started at 2.30 in the morning. The Cistercians were not allowed to sleep afterwards! Their day's work might include copying books or looking after the lay brothers. Unlike the monks, who came from families of the local rich, the lay brothers were probably recruited from illiterate local labourers. They took part in a basic, shortened form of service but were taught skills such as weaving, tanning, carpentry and stonemasonry. They also helped farming sheep at one of thirteen granges owned by the abbey, which by Cistercian rule were within a day's journey of the abbey.

At the abbey itself, hospitality was afforded to travellers, essential in this remote area. Income was also generated with the lay brothers' help as their work was unpaid. Visitors were encouraged by guides across Morecambe Bay. The lay brothers helped in the infirmary that, along with watermills and smithies on the estates, provided services for the community. In return, the needy locals benefited from hospital treatment and charity at the gate. The monks staffed education in schools and acted as priests in chapels further afield. Farmland and churches were granted to the abbey and wealthy patrons subscribed to a rebuilding programme. The Cistercians were thus able to build in their beautiful style of architecture.

This culminated in the magnificent Furness Abbey, whose romantic, idyllic setting and ruins are visible today. You can detect its steady growth in the remains of the nave, cloister, lay brothers' refectory and chapter house. Within a century, the abbey would support a hundred monks and about twice as many lay brothers. It became a place of pilgrimage. Eventually about thirty bishops issued indulgences providing spiritual privileges, such as a relaxation of penances, to people who visited the abbey to venerate an image of the Virgin Mary. It 'mothered' six daughter houses and acquired about 2,000 acres. The mining of iron ore was developed under its control in the Furness area. Other abbeys, like Whalley, second richest in the county, also stimulated prosperity and valuable services for the locality. Leprosy was tended to by specialist hospitals in Lancaster and Preston (and later in Burscough).

VACCARIES

In Medieval times, a journey from the coast of Lancashire into the hills would be an interesting and varied spectacle for the traveller. The bogs and mosses in the wetlands along the coast were barely able to support the subsistence of the occupants but later drainage, such as of the 6-mile-long Martin Mere, encouraged agriculture. The lowland areas were suitable for arable farming on an open field system where narrow strips were allocated to tenants. There might be signs of rotation of crops, as the name Fallowfield near Manchester indicates, but this was not practised as much as in the rest of the country. As the woodland areas further on were cleared, you would see a pattern of irregular fields, scattered farms and hamlets linked by winding lanes.

In the upland areas the landscape scene of the original forest land changed during the Medieval period. At first, they were enjoyed by royalty and nobles for hunting and then enclosed as deer parks, some over 5 miles in circumference. Finally, they were taken over by small-scale commercial farming that bred hardy, long-haired

Traces of vaccaries can be seen near Wycoller. Large, irregular slabs of stone in the fields are probably Medieval and were built as enclosures for cattle to graze on the open hillsides.

cattle in so-called vaccaries. With up to a hundred cattle in each of over fifty vaccaries, it was big business. Their milk could be sold for dairy products and their meat was profitable, too.

Silk from France or Italy

The town life of Lancashire that we know today started to take shape in the twelfth century. Boroughs were created at the lowest point where rivers could be crossed, such as Preston, Lancaster and Warrington. Preston was the first of these to receive a royal charter, from Henry II in 1179. Near Warrington, the Romans had forded the River Mersey at Wilderspool, then two successive wooden bridges were built and destroyed by floods before finally being replaced in stone. The burgesses were exempt from tolls, given control of weights and measures and allowed to set up an independent court. King Edward I gave permission for the town to hold two weekly markets and two annual fairs. In most cases, towns developed from market fairs and trade but Liverpool was different: in 1207 King John wanted a base for his invasion of Ireland.

Imagine livestock crowding the streets. Carts laden with local goods – wool, cheese, hides, barley, salt and fish – rattle on their way to and from the marketplace. Farmers using barns and cowhouses to sell their produce are adding to the variety and congestion. Leather and barrels of beer are transported from micro tanneries and breweries. From further afield, cloth comes from Norfolk, canvas from Galway in Ireland, leather from Spain and you might be lucky to see silk from France or Italy. Most dwellings are single storeyed and some 'under one roof' (semi-detached). The narrow streets and overhanging houses with short frontages belie what lies beyond. Prosperous merchants enjoy gardens, monasteries hide their cemeteries and townsfolk are buried in the graveyard round the parish church.

Black Death

Besides recurrent plagues, life in medieval times was insecure and unpredictable. Famine also threatened along with flooding, Scottish raids, cattle sickness and harvest failures. The Black Death hit Liverpool in the summer of 1349. 'One day people were in high health, and the next day dead and buried.'[7] People might die twelve hours after being infected and usually within three days at the most. Comparatively few of the upper class died; the common people and clergy, the youthful and healthy, suffered most. Whole villages and hamlets were depopulated and left desolate. Irish monk John Clyn thought the end of the world had come: 'I leave my parchment to be continued, in the event that some one of Adam's race may survive the death and wish to continue the work I have begun.'

North Lancashire was particularly affected by the pestilence, which lasted until January 1350. In the south, William of Liverpool was accused of having a the bodies of a third of the inhabitants of Everton, deceased from the plague, delivered to be buried on his lord's property, rather that the 'proper place'.[8] They were carried to his house to be buried as the cemeteries had been overwhelmed. He was extremely fortunate not to have been infected himself.

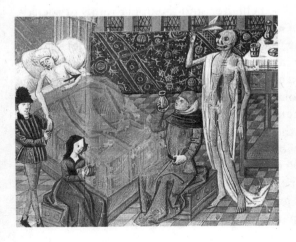

A fifteenth-century miniature personifies a grinning Black Death. The figure towers over powerless mortals and aims a spear at the heart of a rich patient with elaborate hat and tapestries. To no avail, a doctor feels his pulse, a woman prays and a priest prepares the last rites.

The Bishop of Lichfield (in whose diocese south Lancashire fell at that time) allowed the consecration of a graveyard at the chapel of Didsbury. There had been so many dead that it had been impossible to carry them to the parish church at Manchester for burial.

The Black Death affected the relationships between workers and their employers enormously. The agricultural labourer found that he was in demand. Wages rose and the labourers realised that they could set their own price for their work. Soon unreasonable wages were being paid. A law was passed that wages were to be brought down to the level at which they stood before the coming of the pestilence, and that people should not go into the country to help with the harvest, but Lancashire, for some reason, was one of the counties exempt from this.

In the Domesday Book of 1086 it can be calculated that only about 15 per cent of the working force was free, but because of the extra demand for labour particularly after the Black Death, slave and serf numbers decreased to only 1 per cent by the end of the sixteenth century. The position of women in the labour market was also enhanced and their marital prospects, too.

Another outbreak of the plague struck in 1360. The following year, when the country had not yet fully recovered from the first devastation, it afflicted children and the upper ranks of society, including John of Gaunt, the 1st Duke of Lancaster and father of Henry IV. Once again, burial was a problem. Liverpool suffered badly in this outbreak during 1361. The Bishop of Lichfield issued a temporary licence for the burghers to bury the victims at the Chapel of St Nicholas instead of Walton Parish Church.

In 1379 the plague broke out again in the northern counties. At the same time, they were suffering from invasions by the Scots, who seemed oblivious to the risks to which they were exposing themselves. In 1390 there came a recurrence that was so prolonged and so fatal that it can be compared with the Black Death. There were two years of great scarcity, made much worse by six weeks of continual gloom in the second July and August. Superstitiously, the people were sure that the curse of God was upon them. In 1399, they sent a petition to Henry IV praying that he would send assistance because there were not enough able-bodied men left alive to ward off the Scots incursions. When this outbreak ceased, a comparatively long period elapsed before the pestilence came to Lancashire again.

Twenty-four years was a generation in those times, when the average life was much shorter. Many people would know the plague only by repute when it came again in the summer of 1423. The county sessions that were to have been held at Lancaster were adjourned to Preston. This was necessary because the plague was raging in the northern part of the county. Desolation followed as people migrated to avoid contamination.

A Non-Event Starts the War of the Roses

Today, the War of the Roses is conducted on the cricket field and other sporting events. It has its origins in the fifteenth century when the weakness of King Henry VI, ex officio Duke of Lancaster, was challenged by Richard, Duke of York. Shakespeare dramatically pictures this in Part 1, Act 2 of his play *Henry VI*. The Duke of Somerset, cousin of the king and commander of his army, argues Henry's case for the throne with Richard, Duke of York. They ask their followers to choose either a red or white rose to indicate their allegiance to the house of Lancaster or the house of York. In fact, the colours were not strictly adhered to in the war, the term War of the Roses was coined later, and no battle was fought on Lancashire soil. Just a minor incident during the war saw Henry VI captured in Clitheroe Wood as he fled through Lancashire after defeat at Hexham. He was taken to London with his feet tied to the stirrups and lodged in the Tower.

A Lancastrian Turncoat is Richly Rewarded

A prominent Lancashire family played a decisive part in the outcome of the war. In 1385 John Stanley of Storeton in Wirral married Isabel, heiress of Thomas Lathom, one of the richest landowners in the county. The Stanleys and their descendants, the Earls of Derby, played a more significant role in the history of the county than any other family, most of all through their tergiversations.

The first was when John deserted Richard II for Henry of Bolingbroke in 1399. When Henry became King Henry IV, he rewarded John handsomely with estates that, through skilful navigation of turbulent fifteenth-century politics, extended his influence and power. When Richard III seized power, the Stanleys of Lathom and Knowsley supplied him with an army of followers but played an ambivalent role in his Council.

Thomas Stanley, great grandson of John Stanley, had married Margaret Beaufort, mother of Henry Tudor, who fled to France to escape capture. When Henry returned in 1485 to claim the throne, Richard sought to gain Thomas Stanley's military support, holding his son Lord Strange as hostage. Strange escaped, was recaptured and placed under threat of execution if his father failed to add 3,000 soldiers to Richard's side. This would have given overwhelming numbers to Richard. Lord Stanley remarked that he had other sons! When the battle lines at Bosworth Field were drawn up, Stanley stood aside for a while but then committed his troops to join the Lancastrians. Richard charged at Stanley's forces but was killed.

Henry's victory and marriage to Elizabeth of York united the rival claims and ended the war. The sovereign remains the Duke of Lancaster to this day. In gratitude for their help, Henry VII created Stanley Earl of Derby and the family gained great prestige, power and wealth during his reign. The 3rd Earl, Lord Strange, went on to supervise the Dissolution of the Monasteries in Lancashire under Henry VIII. We shall meet the family again in the Civil War, when on that occasion they were steadfast in their loyalty to the crown, as we shall see, to the point of death.

5

TUDOR PEACE AND STUART WAR

Modernise Your House

The Tudor period saw the Lancashire gentry turn their decorated barns into grand houses. Since the fourteenth century, Speke Hall had been inhabited by the Norris family, who extended their estate to land in Lancashire, Cheshire and as far away as Anglesey. Around Speke it was worked by oxen and farmed with dairy herds and flocks of sheep. The Norrises' dwelling went through several phases.

1st Phase

At first, the Norris family probably lived in a simple traditional Medieval hall with a timber frame. It would be heated by an open fire in the centre with the smoke let out through a louvre in the roof. The family might live at one end and be serviced by a kitchen at the other end.

2nd Phase

The first Sir William Norris was knighted for his part in the battle that ended Lambert Simnel's challenge for the throne in 1487. Emboldened by the security this provided, he created a more luxurious hall to enhance his status. At one end, William and his family might dine on a raised dais, maybe with a canopy, and lorded it over visitors of lesser rank and servants. At the other end, or in an adjacent or upper room, the family enjoyed the seclusion of a solar where they could relax and sleep while the servants cosied round the fire.

3RD PHASE

A massive fireplace eventually replaced the traditional hole in the roof. Henry, William's son, distinguished himself at the Battle of Flodden and was content with this accommodation for his small family.

4TH PHASE

His son, the second Sir William, was Mayor of Liverpool, campaigned in Scotland and took part in the sack of Edinburgh in 1544. While there, he stole books from the Royal Library as he was a keen historian and antiquarian. He installed a towering wainscot over the fireplace in the great hall with oak and plaster busts representing Roman emperors. He married twice and had nineteen children. For his growing family, he constructed a Great Parlour, embellishing it with glorious wooden panelling and a richly decorated plaster ceiling that impress and delight visitors to this day. Over the mantelpiece, carved panels proudly depict generations of the family, thirty-three in total (with seven more to come!). A kitchen was built with high windows to prevent the servants from being distracted by looking into the courtyard. They slept in the adjacent roof space, open to the rafters, collar beams and struts.

5TH PHASE

William's son Edward added a bedroom wing with corridors above and below, thus ensuring an unusual degree of privacy. A small round window in the recess to one of the upper-floor chimney stacks acted as a spy hole to warn the Catholic family of undesirable visitors. Another bedroom afforded access to a priest's hole behind panelling.

6TH PHASE

The black and white timber appearance, fashionable at the time, was not rendered until much later, as illustrated on page 54. Nearby in Hale is a much humbler whitewashed cottage with timber frames from the same period. It is reminiscent of pre-medieval buildings, with a thatched roof and a wall infilling of clay-covered wattles. The ingredients for Speke Hall itself were marl, cow dung and chopped straw.

CHETHAM NOT CHEETHAM:
BUSINESSMAN AND PHILANTHROPIST

> All the world's a stage,
> And all the men and women merely players;
> They have their exits and their entrances,
> And one man in his time plays many parts,
> His acts being seven ages ...
>
> Shakespeare, *As You Like It*, Act II, Scene VII

Act I At first the infant, mewling and puking ...
In contrast to the Norrises, Humphrey was born Cheetham in a farmhouse at Crumpsall near Manchester in an enlarged farmhouse in 1580 as illustrated. He started from the humble beginnings of yeoman farmer stock. Who would have thought that he would be commemorated in Manchester to this day?

Act II And then the whining schoolboy ...
Humphrey was educated at Manchester Grammar School. He was one of the earliest cloth merchants who engaged in what was to become a worldwide textile industry. His first step was to rise to the

The final look of Speke Hall after centuries of modernisation. From the left: the Great Parlour (Oak Drawing Room), the Great Hall with its brick chimney over the fireplace, the entrance screen leading through to the courtyard, the Blue Drawing Room and the servants' wing on the right.

Crumpsall Hall, family home of Humphrey Chetham. This may be something like the beginning of Speke Hall.

ranks of the gentry by owning land and employing people to work on his land and serve in the house. The next stage might be an advance to the title of Esquire. 'Cheetham' was reduced to the more refined 'Chetham' but retains its original pronunciation. In the sixteenth century, the Crown made its forest lands available for farming. This attracted outsiders to settle and breed sheep. The cloth was taken to Manchester for sale and export. At first the woollen cloth was of poor quality, but then fustian, a mixture of wool or flax and cotton, was introduced and the cotton was imported through London.

Act III And then the lover ...
He set up business in Manchester while his brother George settled in London to develop a partnership. This was extremely efficient and profitable. Carriers could take the cotton from London to Lancashire and then return with the finished article. He did not marry and gave his wealth away in life and death for good causes.

Act IV Then the soldier ...
The brothers' wealth and prestige increased, and they bought up a number of estates in the troublesome times before and during the Civil War. George died early, but Humphrey continued to invest in buying up family estates, both Royalist and Parliamentarian. When Sir John Radcliffe was imprisoned in the Tower of London in 1627, Turton Tower was the most notable acquisition.

Act V And then the justice ...
Turton Tower was sold after the Restoration, but in the meantime he had funded its Chapel, Bolton Church and the Collegiate Church of Manchester. In 1634 he was appointed Sheriff of the county. This was not just an honour but involved enforcing the law and dressing himself and servants in expensive livery. For several years he had been 'Farmer of the Manchester Tithes', when he was in charge of gathering in the tithes, not in kind but in money. As Sheriff, he was expected to collect 'Ship Money' for the Crown, which he carried out efficiently and fairly.

Act VI The sixth age shifts into the lean and slippered pantaloon ... In the Civil War Humphrey was appointed treasurer of the county committee for raising money for the Parliamentary cause. In 1648, at the age of 69, he resigned but within weeks was reappointed. His appeal against the decision on account of his age was accepted.

Act VII Last scene of all, that ends this strange eventful history ... When Humphrey died at home in Clayton Hall in 1653 he was the richest man in the north of England and the value of his estate on death would make him a multimillionaire today. During his lifetime he had made provision for the maintenance of twenty-two poor boys. In his will he provided for the purchase of a college building and ordained that the number should be increased to forty. They would be given an education from the age of 6 to 14 to prepare them for an apprenticeship. He also donated books and money for the creation of the first free library in England. It is the oldest surviving public library in Britain and one in which Marx and Engels studied. The school buildings, dating from 1421, had been built to accommodate a college of priests attached to the church (now the cathedral) and form part of the present day Chetham's School of Music.

Humphrey should be celebrated as the first successful businessman to create a fortune and give it away to good causes. He was also instrumental in establishing a new process for buying and selling cloth. Before his time, the cloth had been woven independently in the home. It was transformed into a system acting between suppliers and producers that extended through Manchester to the rest of the country and through Liverpool to the rest of the world. He was historically an important figure at the very start of Manchester's evolution into 'cottonopolis', which epitomised the first industrial society in the world.

WILLING AND UNWILLING WITCHES

At the beginning of the seventeenth century, Lancastrians were used to dealing with the misfortunes of disease, floods, harvest failure and personal tragedies. No wonder they were ready to blame anyone they thought might be responsible and seek religious and magical remedies. Such is the background to the infamous tragedy of the Pendle witches. Their leader or Witch Queen, Old Demdike or Elizabeth Southernes, proclaimed that her powers came from her alliance with someone she called a devil or spirit, who offered her anything she wished in exchange for her soul. She and others had met as a 'coven' for fifty years, sometimes merry making, sometimes forming conspiracies. They dressed in animal masks and practised primitive worship. Their familiar spirits would be black cats, toads or other animals that appeared in the eyes of the witches as an embryonic devil. They took pride in their supposed evil powers and boasted of the death of a cow and the bewitching of a man's drink.

In 1612, one of His Majesty's Justices, Roger Nowell, decided it was his duty to root out this coven for the honour of Lancashire. When he questioned the coven, they eagerly admitted that they were witches and were summoned for trial at the Assizes at Lancaster Castle. Within a week their friends gathered at Malking Tower, their usual meeting place, and decreed that the Gaoler of Lancaster Castle should be slain and the castle blown up. They were promptly arrested and imprisoned there.

During their trial the witches insisted on their own guilt even when a sure penalty of death faced them for the confession. They may have believed that their familiar spirits would rescue them at the last minute. Five of the witches brought to trial pleaded guilty. Old Demdike died in prison and the other four were executed. Five others who pleaded innocent and refused to make confession were also executed at Golgotha near Lancaster. The case raised great interest locally as many of them were known personally, and also nationally as one of those executed was a 'gentlewoman'. Great play was made of this 'sin' for many years.

Just over twenty years later, in 1634, another case arose in nearby Whalley. A boy, Edmund Robinson, was brought before the magistrates with a story explaining why he had been late home from school. He had met two greyhounds that turned into two human beings, a female neighbour and a boy. The woman then turned the boy into a black horse and carried Edmund with her on the horse to a witches' Sabbath. His story bore a resemblance to the accounts of the Pendle witches with details of the devil who wore a cloven hoof, and of witches who sat up in the chimney or stuck thorns into pictures. His father, also Edmund, vouched for him and others came forward with similar experiences, accusing the supposed witches, and one woman testified against herself. At the Lancaster assizes that followed, seventeen of the witches were found guilty by the jury, but they were reprieved and the matter was referred to King Charles I and the Privy Council.

When the sensational news reached London, the king summoned them, and Edmund, father and son, to attend him. Of the seven chosen by the king, three had already died, so four were handed from sheriff to sheriff on the way to London. After fifteen months in Lancaster Gaol, one of them was sick and despairing, another indignant at false accusations and malicious neighbours, the third wished for death after seeing her mother and father die in the gaol, and the last was 60 years old, penitent and weeping for her sins as a witch. The bewildered four were examined unsuccessfully for witches' marks on their bodies, lodged at the Ship Tavern in Greenwich and then put on show in Fleet Prison for an expensive entrance fee. Edmund Robinson, son, was re-examined and confessed that he had made up the story to avoid a beating from his father for being late home from school. Edmund Robinson, father, maintained he had in good faith believed his son and intended no malice. A comedy play was popular for a while making fun of the witches as characters, but the reality was that they were still in Lancaster Gaol two years later.

Ironically, the term Lancashire Witch lived on almost as a term of pride. 'The Lancashire Novelist' Harrison Ainsworth, born in Manchester and friend and contemporary of Dickens, wrote his most enduring historical novel *The Lancashire Witches*. George Stephenson built a locomotive, the first of a new breed, for the Bolton & Leigh Railway, a freight line opened two years before the Liverpool & Manchester Railway. At the opening ceremony it was named *Lancashire Witch* and decorated with a garland of roses and other flowers. However, to foreigners the name still conveyed a sinister connotation. Ten years later, in 1838, visiting traveller William Howitt described in his *Rural Life of England* the women of the district as 'of stalwart and masculine feature and of a hardness of feature which gives them no claim to be ranked among the most dangerous of the Lancashire Witches'.

King v Parliament

More decisive action took place in Lancashire during the Civil War than any other county and the first blood is said to have been shed in Bury. Lancastrians were also riven by acute religious differences. At the outbreak of the war, Lancashire gentry were strongly Catholic and therefore Royalist.

When the war broke out in 1642, the Royalists' initial prime objective was to secure the military magazines at the main towns of Lancaster, Preston, Liverpool and Manchester. They succeeded in all except Manchester and, when the Parliamentarians of the town attempted a peaceful settlement in Bury, a brawl broke out. But tensions remained and came to a head when Lord Strange, 7th Earl of Derby, called for a great meeting on Preston Moor, which was accompanied by a nearby gathering of Parliamentarians. Shouts 'for the king' were opposed by 'King and Parliament' while the town's gunpowder supply was being spirited away by the Royalists. In the lawlessness that followed, each side elected a mayor of its own. Lord Derby attacked Manchester and raised money for his war effort. His army was recruited from old country people armed with pitchforks. They were encouraged from the rear by troopers ordered to shoot those who lagged behind.

The following year (1643) the Parliamentarians advanced from Blackburn and regained control of Preston. However, Lord Derby raised a large force in the Royalist Fylde and marched on Lancaster. When the town refused to surrender, it is related that his soldiers would not attack a second time but Derby, seized a short pike and sprang forward, calling out 'follow me'. Some gentlemen volunteers immediately joined him and urged the soldiers on. The assault was made, the city taken and the fortifications razed. It was sacked and burned, but the garrison was barricaded in the castle. When a Parliamentarian force set out from Preston to relieve the garrison, Derby neatly sidestepped it and captured Preston completely by surprise. He was greeted with shouts of 'God bless the King and the Earl of Derby'.

A Brave Lancashire Lass

His triumph was short-lived. Setting out to attack the Parliamentarian forces in Blackburn, he was in turn surprised and defeated by the enemy. Fleeing from the field on horseback, he retired to the Isle of Man to forestall a revolt there against the king. His wife, Charlotte, Countess of Derby, was left behind to defend Lathom House, one of the family properties. It was attacked by the Parliamentarians, who were led by a senior commander, Thomas Fairfax. Although faced with forces six times larger than her own, she took the offensive by sorties from the house into the enemy camp. After the destruction inflicted by one of these, Fairfax was reduced to declaring a day of fasting and prayer in his camp. Six times she was offered surrender on varying terms, but she rejected them scornfully, once threatening to hang the messenger. The siege was lifted when Prince Rupert approached with overwhelming forces and took control of Lancashire. The earl and countess were free for a jubilant and emotional reunion, albeit a short-lived one.

Lancashire suffered grievously in the Civil War. Lancaster had been burnt to the ground; Bolton had been sacked and 1,600 died in a massacre; in Liverpool, 360 had been killed in Rupert's attack. The outcome of the 'First' Civil War was decided by Rupert's defeat in 1644 at Marston Moor in Yorkshire. The Parliamentarians returned to besiege Lathom House – and this time, it capitulated.

CHARLES, JAMES, JACOBITES AND CHARLIE

The Civil War was reignited by a second one in 1648 when a Scottish army invaded England in support of the king. They did not endear themselves to the local people by rustling their cattle and were defeated by Oliver Cromwell's New Model Army, first at Ribbleton Moor near Preston and then at Winwick Pass as they straggled along between Preston and Warrington.

King Charles was executed the following year but his son, the future Charles II, landed in Scotland 1651 in an attempt to regain the throne for the Stuarts. He advanced through Lancashire with his army and the Earl of Derby hastened with 700 Manx soldiers from the Isle of Man to join him. On the way, he visited his deserted and desolate Lathom House.

The joint forces defeated the Parliamentarians at Warrington. The main force marched south to Worcester, but the earl was sent back to raise reinforcements for the cause in Lancashire. Leading his troops by night to loyal Wigan, he was met by a Parliamentarian contingent. In the fierce fight that ensued, the earl's horse was twice shot from under him, and he received seven shots on his breastplate and thirteen cuts on the beaver of his helmet. Parliament voted official thanks for their victory, but the earl escaped to join in the Battle of Worcester. After the Royalist defeat there, he saw the king to safety but was captured on his way north, tried for treason and condemned to execution in Bolton. This was where the Bolton Massacre had taken place in 1644 when the Royalists allegedly killed as many as 1,600 Parliamentarian defenders and inhabitants after storming the town under Prince Rupert. The Stanley/Derbys lost most of their estates except for Lathom and Knowsley and the countess was imprisoned in the Isle of Man. On the restoration of Charles II as king in 1660, the earl's son and his wife were able to return to the Derby estates. However, the dominance that the family had exerted over Lancashire since the Tudors had been broken.

For a while, the Stuart cause was in the ascendant. In 1688 James II arrived at Preston on his way to Hoghton Tower. He was welcomed with a speech at the cross, presented with a bowl and feted at the town hall. At Hoghton a stag was hunted and killed, and he dined at the lord's table. Doubtless he was reminded of an earlier visit by his grandfather James I in 1617. Sir Richard Hoghton had given him literal red carpet treatment by laying one along the half-mile avenue leading to the house. The story goes that the king was delighted with his beef steak and dubbed it Sir Loin, hence sirloin!

The Royalists surreptitiously fostered anti-Whig sentiment in towns such as Preston by the formation of a mock corporation that feasted in style with offices of House-groper, Slut-kisser, Custard-eater and others. The town seems to have been a magnet for battles that were decisive, and lost, in the Royalist cause. In 1715, a Scottish army was mobilised in support of 'the Old Pretender' 'King James III' and occupied Lancaster. Here the gallant Jacobites were royally entertained by the ladies of the town before entering Preston and proclaiming James as king. However, while they were enjoying themselves, the government troops gathered and crossed the river from the south. There ensued battles in the streets and houses. Fires were started to force the 'Highlanders' out of the blazing buildings. The arrival of overwhelming government forces persuaded the Scots to surrender unconditionally.

Preston was considered hostile territory and the soldiers had to be stopped from plundering the town. Savage reprisals were taken against the locals. Those who had joined the enemy were tried before a special government commission in Liverpool. Twelve men were hanged in Preston and four in Garstang with their heads exposed for public view.

Although this seemed to have eclipsed Stuart hopes, thirty years later in 1745, Bonnie Prince Charlie, the 'Young Pretender' to the British throne, advanced with an army from Scotland and lodged in the town. Some veterans superstitiously remembered that thirty years before they had failed to cross the Ribble, so a few of them were stationed on the south side of the river. Some Catholics, including Francis Towneley, welcomed Charlie, but the local authorities maintained a careful diplomatic middle course then, and again when Charlie returned after his defeat at Derby. Francis was executed for supporting the rebellion.

A Cavalier's Note Book

During the Civil War, Lancashire Catholics supported the king, which made them the enemy twice over of the Puritan Parliamentarians. William Blundell, 'the Cavalier' of Crosby, wrote in his notebook that the Parliamentarians would raid any suspect Catholic house and carry off 'anything they could lay their hands on, that they [the Catholics] were obliged to bury their bread from meal to meal'. William's thigh had been shattered with a musket shot in Lord Derby's taking of Lancaster at the beginning of the Civil War. He recovered from the serious wound thanks to a week's devoted nursing, but was crippled for

A list of army ranks and a doodle of a Cavalier from the Great Hodge Podge, a manuscript volume of the Blundell family containing odds and ends of data from Elizabethan to Victorian days. It was started by William the Recusant, grandfather of William the Cavalier. (Courtesy Mark Blundell)

life, earning him the nickname 'Halt-Will' and having to wear a 3in-high heel to maintain his height.

The family suffered grievously under the penal laws inflicted on them during the Commonwealth. William was forced to seek refuge in his friends' houses and leave the family home in the care of his wife or sister. During this time, a resident priest was hidden away in the upper part of the house but had to be on the alert for capture at the mercy of informers. William was imprisoned four times, the last in 1657 at Liverpool in a 'loathsome prison' for ten weeks. His estate was seized by the Commissioners for ten years and his wife bought a horse and two oxen to make a team and farm the land. In the end, with the help of two Protestant friends, he repurchased the estate, which was heavily in debt.

Later, he escorted two of his daughters to safety in France to lead a religious life. The journey there proved most uncomfortable and hazardous with storms on the sea and accidents on the road. In contrast, he was present to welcome Charles II back to British shores. The restoration of the monarchy allowed him to renew his pleasures of hunting and horse racing on the Crosby course. He compiled commonplace books of interesting events of his times and places he visited. His social life included the visit of Barbara Villiers, mistress of Charles II, to the bowling green at nearby Sefton, a far cry from court life in London. He travelled widely through Britain and to Ireland and France.

This peaceful life was interrupted in 1680 when sixty-four leading Lancashire Catholics were identified on a list for banishment but William volunteered to go abroad for a while instead. When William of Orange intended to invade in 1688, William Blundell suggested an ineffectual plan of sharp-tipped rods that could impale the enemy cavalry. So, on the new king's 'Glorious Revolution' the following year, he was not surprisingly imprisoned for a fifth time at Manchester for nine weeks, but was comforted by the 'cheerful society' of fellow prisoner Charles Townley. On release, however, he was confined to within 5 miles of his house for the remainder of his life so that he could not join in any movement to restore James II. This interlude passed uneventfully until 5.30 a.m. on 30 July 1694, when three of the king's messengers invaded the hall at Crosby. As William was then 74 years old, he was not arrested but his son was taken away on the spot and later escorted to London and imprisoned in Newgate to be accused of participation in the 'Lancashire Plot'. He was acquitted by the judge with the biblical warning to 'go and sin no more'. William the Cavalier lived out the rest of his days at Crosby Hall and died there in 1698.

Puritan and Dissenter

The career of Henry Newcombe illustrates the difficulties faced by someone from the other end of the religious spectrum during this turbulent time. After several incumbencies in Cheshire, Henry was called to the Collegiate Church in Manchester (now the cathedral) in 1657 but soon became a member of the Presbyterian regional body. In spite of his Puritan background, he enjoyed the pleasures allowed by the restoration of Charles II in 1660. He even played bandy ball, a form of tennis, on Sundays and also shuffleboard, although he condemned the associated heavy drinking, and he did not object to schoolchildren having the day off on Shrove Tuesday for sports and cock fighting. He continued to preach in the church until the Conventicle Act of 1664 and the obligation to use the Anglican prayer book. This he refused to ascribe to, and he was penalised by the Five Mile Act into moving away to Rochdale, where he stayed with a friend. Illegally, he visited his family and other friends and prayed with them. Once he was surprised by the visit of 'chimney lookers' for the assessment of the hearth tax but escaped discovery. He preached in barns and other secret locations. Short of money, he was not able to set Dan, one of his sons, up in business. Sacrificing his Puritan ideals, Henry apprenticed him to a ribbon manufacturer in London. When Dan ran away, he was sent to Jamaica but returned home when he contracted yellow fever there.

Dissenters' hopes were lifted by the Declaration of Indulgence of Charles II in 1672, which allowed them freedom of worship, but Parliament forced him to withdraw it. Henry's money problems were alleviated by his brothers, who funded the education of two of his other sons at Cambridge. Twice, his house was searched, during the Rye House Plot of 1683 and the Monmouth Rebellion of 1685, but nothing incriminating was found. The accession of William and Mary in 1688 and defeat of James II in Ireland brought welcome relief to nonconformists and in 1693 Henry's congregation built him a handsome 'Dissenters' Meeting House' in Cross Street, Manchester. However, he died two years later, worn out at the age of 68 by thirty years of trials and tribulations. Cross Street was the mother church of nonconformity in Manchester and during the eighteenth century became a Unitarian chapel. The modern chapel is the third on the site as the original building, destroyed during the war, has since been rebuilt twice.

Proud Protestant Preston

In contrast to Henry Newcombe's fluctuating fortunes, the local Protestant gentry of Preston were enjoying a busy and varied social life. The diary of Captain Bellingham records bull baiting, playing bowls, carousing and frequenting inns and coffee houses.

Dr Kuerden was born in Cuerden and educated at the nearby grammar school in Leyland and then at Oxford and Cambridge. In a detailed work based on contemporary official records, he describes a prosperous port and market town in the late seventeenth century serving a wide area. Quarterly sessions were held for the administration of justice for the local hundred (district) of Amounderness and of Blackburn.

Market provision was supplied separately for butchers, dairy products, corn, fish, cattle, pigs, leather, cloth and hardware. Salmon could be fished from the River Ribble and travel to London expedited by a fine stone bridge (at Walton).

A 'large and handsome' school stood alongside a well-built church. Hospitals, alms houses and a workhouse helped the sick and poor. Away from the town centre, the ruins of an old priory had been converted into a House of Correction. Here, the prisoners were put to hard labour on a restricted diet and punished by a whipping chair. They might emerge 'with a naked and bloody farewell' for transportation elsewhere.

6

GEORGIAN INNOVATION AND CHANGE

Merely Draining

Today you cannot imagine Rufford Old Hall perched on a low eminence near a huge expanse of water. But it used to be on the edge of Martin Mere, one of the largest bodies of fresh water in the county, about 14 miles in perimeter. The name of the hall came from the 'rough ford' that crossed the drainage channel leading from the mere to the River Douglas. Dugout boats from much earlier times have been recovered but from the twelfth century rights over the lake had been held by the priors of Burscough. On the dissolution of the monasteries, the rights were transferred to local landed families: the Earls of Derby in Lathom, the Scarisbricks of Scarisbrick Hall and the Heskeths, who derived their name from the Viking word for 'horse racing course'. Later on, they would marry into the Fleetwood family and be prominent in Southport. At that time, the mere was frequented by fish of all kinds – roach, eels, pike, perch and bream – and by geese and swans. Significantly, even the servants in the great hall at Rufford enjoyed the luxury of feather bolsters, pillows and mattresses.

Martin Mere was the first of the many mosslands in Lancashire to be drained, and the largest. In the 1690s, Thomas Fleetwood obtained a lease from the other proprietors. It was to last for two lives plus thirty-one years for completion of the work. Unfortunately, this period was considerably shortened when Fleetwood and his daughter died within two years of each other. Fleetwood first cut a channel or sluice from the mere to the Ribble Estuary, employing, it is said, as many as 2,000 men in the dry season. It was 24ft wide and deep enough to drain the water away from the mere. Flood gates were then constructed, which were closed at high tide to prevent the sea water flowing into the mere but open at other times to keep it drained. It was an immediate success and the rich reclaimed land was used for agriculture. Although the traveller Celia Fiennes was apprehensive of the notorious dangers of the area and avoided them, she appreciated the industry and expense devoted to the project.

However, a court case was brought by people whose livelihood had been affected. Witnesses attested that they had lost grazing lands and could not harvest reeds for thatch or take wildfowl and their eggs. Sands from the Ribble Estuary drifted into the outfall. The cure of raising the sill at the floodgate by 20in was counteracted by the lack of drainage.

When Fleetwood died, he was buried in nearby Churchtown. His monument (translated from the Latin) says, 'He wished his bones to be here laid because he made into dry and firm land the great Martinensian Marsh ... He likewise constructed, not far off, a handsome bridge over the estuary at no small cost, from a regard rather to the public good than to his own prospective advantage.' After Fleetwood's death, a new pair of floodgates improved the situation but in 1754 an unusually high tide washed these away.

A deteriorating situation caused by neglect was to some extent alleviated by Thomas Eccleston, who took over the Scarisbrick estate in 1778. As the largest landowner on the mere, he had begun to take an interest in the problem. He deepened the main drainage channel and fitted new lock gates. This enabled extra land to be tilled for crops of wheat, barley and hay for the breeding of coach horses and cattle. For this, Eccleston won a gold medal from the Society for the Encouragement of Arts Manufactures and Commerce in 1786. Part of the old mere is now the site of the Martin Mere Wetland Centre.

Only One Day Missed in Nearly Six Thousand

From 1702 to 1728 Nicholas Blundell wrote an entry in his diary every day, except one. He was the grandson of William Blundell, the Cavalier and Lord of the Manor of Crosby Hall. In the second year of entries, he describes how he made a five-day journey to Gloucestershire to meet Frances, daughter of Lord Langdale, who was the grandson of the Royalist general Marmaduke Langdale. They married two months later.

Wisely, or maybe characteristically, he kept to himself after the Catholic misfortunes in the Civil War and for the most part led a quiet gentleman farmer's life. He was on friendly terms with the local Anglican rector of Sefton Church, but from 1707 harboured a priest for twenty-one years who was referred to as Mr (Robert) Aldred, both in person and in the diary, to disguise his real identity as Catholics were still not safe. At first Aldred lived in the hall but, because there was friction between him and Frances, he transferred to a cottage in the village. Mass was celebrated secretly for the family and villagers. At the height of persecution Aldred visited nearby Ince Blundell Hall and enjoyed country pursuits, especially coursing, to the full but he would often be forced to hide in the priest's hole at Crosby Hall while Frances hid the vestments and sacred vessels in the 'false roof'. Besides the cottage and an allowance, he received 'considerable' financial assistance from the yeomen and farmers, who were all Catholics.

Aldred was the diarist's closest friend. Such diverse subjects as fattening cattle and the celibacy of priests were discussed with him and he helped Nicholas to settle quarrels. Later, a 'house' was built for him with a chapel in the hall grounds near the village. It was probably the first Roman Catholic chapel to be built in England since the Reformation. As it was being built, the alarm was raised when a customs officer descended with a constable to check on smuggled goods. Nicholas, Aldred and the local gentry were part of a consortium dealing in claret and brandy, but they escaped detection. Nicholas designed and supervised the building himself and celebrated its completion with 'a good bowl of Punsh' (no doubt made of contraband brandy!).

Suspected of implication in the 1715 Jacobite Rebellion, Nicholas escaped to Flanders for two years, where he visited his numerous relations and friends. On his return, Nicholas resumed his devotion to the estate, laying out formal gardens and renovating the house. He also developed a brickworks, making hundreds of thousands of bricks to sell, as well as for his own use building on the estate. He describes the daily activities about the house, on the farm and in the garden, and the work, amusements and troubles of his tenants and labourers. He recorded his business and social engagements, his pastimes, the visits he and his family made, the comings and goings of friends and the medical treatments prescribed, observing anything of interest in normal daily activity as well as any unusual events.

A particularly important activity was marling: extracting marl, a kind of limey clay that breaks up very easily, and was highly valued as a fertiliser for its property of improving light sandy soils in particular. Marlers went in groups from one estate to another, contracting with the landowner to bore for the clay, dig it out, and spread it in the agreed proportion on the selected land. The lord of the manor would notify some of his tenants that he required them and their horses and carts for marling. This was one of the boon duties the tenants had to perform as part of their rent for the lord of the manor. The workers were given free beer and meat in addition to their pay. The cost was well worthwhile in the greater yield of crops from the marled field. One curious custom in connection with marling was that of 'shouting'. Blundell, in his diary, tells us frequently that when he took friends to see the marlers at work he made the marlers 'to shout', and for this entertainment the visitors gave the marlers ale or 2s 6d towards the cost of the festivities. So they were 'shouting' for their ale (the term survives in Australian slang). When completed, the marl pit would be 'flowered' with decorations of all kinds. The celebrations went on for several days with dancing in the hall and in the barn to the music of pipes and fiddles while the home-brewed brown ale flowed freely in the light of candles and rushes. The marl pits often created a pond or mere, so traces of them can be seen to this day. The boulder stone that started this history was unearthed in a marl pit.

BLACKPOOL COULD HAVE BEEN LIVERPOOL

Blackpool took its name from a dark-coloured pool from which a 'liver-coloured' stream ran to the seashore. In the early eighteenth century on the northern, Bispham, side of the pool stood a mansion, the home of the Tyldesleys, an old Lancashire country family. Thomas Tyldesley, who was living there in the early eighteenth century, kept a diary that paints a vivid picture of the life of an easy-going country squire of the time. He was fond of gardening (an early cultivator of 'pottatows') in the area. He enjoyed cock fighting, angling and hunting foxes, fowl and otters. He built himself a schooner to trade with the Isle of Man (maybe to smuggle goods) and profited from a coal mine. He enjoyed smoking a clay pipe with tobacco obtained from Preston and kept a varied diet of fresh and locally sourced fresh fish, meat, fruit and vegetables.

His life was hugely different from the handful of fisher families whose huts and cabins on the cliffs overlooked the sea. Their low cottages were built with crook frames, wattle and daub walls and thatch roofs. The rafters, blackened by the fire, stored dried fish, bacon and salt beef. Cut off from the outside world, these families were highly superstitious, with their own guttural dialect. The women wore distinctive dress: a white or red homespun jacket and skirt for working days, but on holidays their dress would be embellished with fringes, coloured stomachers and beribboned hats.

In the 1750s bathers could be accommodated at 'Black Pool', close to a few prospective lime kilns. The hamlet, a village without shops, was graced only by Forshaw's Hotel. But, by the

Blackpool in 1760. Such buildings encouraged a variety of popular activities during the day: archery, bathing, bowling and sailing. In the evenings you could amuse yourself with playing cards, drinking at taverns or reading books from a public library.

end of the century, Lane Ends Inn was advertised for sale with stabling, 'any quantity of land from 12 to 30 acres' and seventy beds. Favourite amusements consisted of walking along the shore and strolling on the grass Parade alongside it, 6 yards wide and 200 yards long. It was a beauty parade too, with the gentlemen in short breeches, buckled shoes and cornered hats, and the ladies in flowery silk or cotton skirts and elegant high coiffures.

Visitors came by post coach from Manchester and excursions could be made to Preston Races and Wigan Spa by roads only recently paved. The threshing floor of a barn, with rows of benches representing the pit and gallery, formed a makeshift theatre with a capacity of about ninety and prices of 2s and 1s (£12 and £6 today) respectively. A bell summoned the ladies to bathe in horse-drawn machines. On the toll of a second bell, the ladies retired and the gentlemen plunged in. Horse rides of 20 miles could be enjoyed along the sands at low tide. Fast forward to 1846 and the first mill outing arrived from Swinton. Another leap lands you in 'Las Vegas of the North'.

Travel, Collect and Display your Treasures

A tour of the Continent was essential for the aristocracy in the eighteenth century, especially to Italy to complete their classical education. The Towneley family, with their home near Burnley, had been loyal to their faith and the king since about 1200, and suffered for it. Francis was executed following his support for the Jacobite Rebellion of 1745. However, Charles Townley (as he now spelt the family name) revived the family fortunes and between 1765 and 1777 he travelled on three Grand Tours to Italy buying hundreds of art treasures. To display his collection, he bought a fashionable Georgian house in London overlooking St James' Park near Buckingham House (later Palace).

Charles was bisexual and did not marry. On his death the collection was purchased by the British Museum, where it resides, surpassed only by Lord Elgin's Marbles. Towneley Hall, begun about 1400, was acquired by Burnley Council in 1901 and is now their art gallery and museum.

Like Charles Townley, Henry Blundell of Ince Blundell Hall near Liverpool travelled widely on the Continent. He built up a collection of classical statues and housed them in a replica of the Pantheon in Rome. When the family died out, his collection was given to the Walker Art Gallery in Liverpool, but his Pantheon survives, unadorned and bereft of its treasures.

Another collector was John Foster Junior, whose father was Chief Surveyor of Liverpool and wanted to give him the best architectural education. However, as it was during the time of the Napoleonic Wars, John Junior could not visit Italy because of the French occupation. Travelling to Greece instead, he acquired copies of ancient sculptures for his hometown and, as Chief Surveyor of Liverpool in his turn, established there an enduring Greek revival style of architecture.

When is the Next High Tide?

It is difficult to appreciate these days the incomparable difficulties in navigating the coasts of Britain in the eighteenth century. The tides in the Mersey Estuary were some of the highest on the coast of Britain – and there was no perfectly accurate information with which to predict them.

William Hutchinson worked his way up from being a cabin boy on Merchant Navy ships to be appointed Dockmaster of the Liverpool Docks in 1759, a position he held for forty years. He was, incidentally, an inventor. He studied scientific shipbuilding through the observation of miniature ships, devised pioneering reflecting mirrors for Bidston Lighthouse on the Wirral in 1763 and experimented with artificial respiration.

He arranged for the first lifeboat station in Britain to be established in Formby in the early 1770s. Liverpool Corporation paid for a sailor to be appointed to take care of a boat and boat house. He and the boat's crew would be 'handsomely rewarded hereafter for such good service done herein and not less than one guinea per head for every life or person they shall save'[9] (about £160 today). The lifeboat was the only one serving the harbour until 1803, when other Liverpool Bay stations were established. William had personal experience of shipwrecks, enduring very narrow escapes himself.

He began compiling records of tides in Liverpool in 1768 and continued every day until 1793, that is, for 'twenty-five years, seven months and ten days' (you can hear the perfection of his recording). William Whewell, Master of Trinity College, Cambridge, 1841–56, and a central figure in Victorian science, heard of his researches and used them in a debate in which he was involved about tide predictions. He was exuberant to find they proved he was correct. Through connections with Hutchinson, Liverpool tidologists created tide timetables that were by far the most accurate in the country, taking into account the diurnal inequality, that is the variable distance in height between one tide and the next one in the day.

There is a memorial to Hutchinson which marks the boundary of the Old Dock in Liverpool, the first commercial dock in the world, constructed between 1710 and 1716. A series of water jets are accompanied by inscriptions of the measurements of the height and times of high water at the dock, which William took during January 1783.

SUGAR SLAVERY

In 1565 an Irish ship carrying raw sugar was wrecked on the southern shore of the Ribble Estuary. The local inhabitants of North Meols commandeered the cargo and set up some 'sugar houses' to refine it. At the time sugar was a luxury, on a par with exotic spices. Following the Great Fire of London in 1666, merchants dealing with the north-west weighed up the expense of rebuilding there with the added costs of transportation by the lengthy and dangerous circuit round Land's End and Wales. An alternative was to receive shipments in Lancashire directly from the plantations and refine there, especially in ports. Ready availability of coal and water for the process was an added attraction. From the 1670s refineries sprouted on a commercial scale in Liverpool and imports of raw sugar increased seventyfold during the 1700s for manufacture there and onward distribution to be refined in Warrington, Manchester and Chester. Even Ormskirk, 12 miles away from Liverpool with heavy transport costs by muddy roads, refined its own sugar for a while in the 1670s.

To start with, raw sugar came from Madeira or the Canary Islands. Later on, Caribbean plantation owners decided they could make more money by growing sugar cane instead of tobacco, and imports were channelled through the ports of Liverpool, Preston and Lancaster. Demand for the product grew, together with a dearth of labour to produce it. In 1648 Liverpool Borough Council rounded up poor children and beggars from the streets and sent them to Barbados as indentured servants, tantamount to slavery. They were also offered to ships' captains to endure the same fate. However, when a yellow fever epidemic killed half the population of Barbados in the middle of the seventeenth century, the plantation owners turned to enslaved Africans instead. A century later, black Americans accounted for most of the population of some southern states of America because of their immunity to malaria. Ultimately, as many as 12 million Africans were to be transported across the Atlantic.

Captains, traders and merchants were happy to embark on the hateful enterprise to secure the vast profits in spite of the financial risks involved. For example, in 1702 a Lancaster merchant invested in a ship (called the *Imployment*!) bound for Barbados. It returned with a cargo of sugar, molasses and ginger. As England was at war with France (and there was danger from pirates), the ship sailed in convoy for safety, but became separated from the rest and was captured by the French. The captain offered himself as a hostage for a huge ransom if the ship was allowed to continue under his mate, but the mate ran it aground on Rossall Point. Although the ship was a wreck, most of the cargo was salvaged. Happily (for some) the French accepted an offer of half of the original ransom money (over £100,000 today) and the investor continued to trade.

After the Jacobite Rebellion of 1745, the government was embarrassed by the large number of prisoners. They were offered a choice: they could hang for treason or confess their guilt and be deported to the sugar fields. Women and children chose first, the rest were chosen by lot. One Liverpool sugar refiner with previous experience of transporting human cargoes was contracted to take 936 across the Atlantic at £5 per head. There, they would be sold on to plantation owners for indentures at £7 per head, making a potential profit for him of the equivalent of well over £1 million today.[10] Some of the prisoners who had to be brought from a distance were incarcerated in tiny Liverpool cells or in the holds of hulks in the docks. Others, shackled in irons, were drowned in the Mersey when their boat capsized on transfer to a large one. It was two years before a small vessel, crammed full and named *Gildart* after the contractor, set sail with forty-seven prisoners for the Caribbean. More hell ships followed.

PSYCHEDELIC FIRESIDE

'May they enjoy health and happiness and have the comfort of a son in nine months is the wish of all present' and 'George Bates hath paid one shilling in ale for ye honour of having a daughter launched at half past eleven o'clock last night'. These are two of over a thousand entries in a unique record: the minutes of a social club in Georgian Liverpool. The club met each evening at an ale house called The Three Tuns in what is now the Strand, close to the docks. It was frequented by sea captains and local tradesmen who assembled to discuss matters of great or little importance and consumed ale by the 'nipperkin'. They imagined themselves as being governed by Aeolus, Greek god of the wind, and sold his favour to intending seafarers. Their bets were happily spent on the ale consumed at the gathering.

A series of entries starting 25 November 1776 recorded that 'Captain George Water has paid one shilling for a fair wind for the ship Hope, may she have a prosperous voyage, which is the wish of all present'; then, 'Not authorised by Aeolus therefore the ship returned this December.' And on 11 December, 'Captain John Hewett has paid two shillings for a fair wind purchased from the original Aeolus.'

Most of the ale was paid for in fines for new suits of clothes. The bright colours of the Georgian cartoonists of the period were no exaggeration. The gaudy appearance of those attending excited passionate descriptions and we can imagine a fair sprinkling of these general colours at any meeting: claret, damson, pea green, toad's back or sage green (lined with white silk), 'brown big coat with a green collar', and 'damned ugly green'! Others were enhanced by buttons: chocolate coloured with gilt buttons; blue with oval yellow buttons; dark brown with death's head buttons of the same colour; green and orange with buttons of the same; Devonshire brown with macaroni buttons; purple olive coloured with yellow buttons; dirty grey with large diamond buttons. Some really pushed the boat out with eye-catching combinations (imagine one yourself!):

> purple coat, green striped waistcoat, white metal buttons
> thunder and lightning coat, hell-fire waistcoat, and black breeches
> dark orange and green coat, white waistcoat, and black silk breeches

Many superstitious and hopeful bets were placed on successful voyages: 'Captain Johnston lays Mr Thomas Cartmell one guinea to one shilling that Ralph Fisher Captain of the Charles Town has not sold two cargoes of slaves since he left Liverpool in the West Indies and America.' Besides this most profitable and repellent trade, interests ranged from whalers in the Arctic to Cheshire cheese on its way to London. During this time of the American War of Independence, there were wagers on the truth or falsehood of news reported in the campaign. Current events for good or evil are recorded: a huge win in the National Lottery, 'Drawn a prize of £20,000, the property of Dillon and Leyland of this town.' This money (worth £2.5 million today[11]) was used to found a bank, now part of HSBC. Curious bets were laid: 'that there is a single seat in St Mary's Church that will hold eight women' and 'that a first-rate ship of war from the keel to the top-gallant mast head is not so high as St Thomas's Church Steeple' (216ft, later shortened to 198ft when a hurricane blew down 42ft of its height).

Women are only mentioned incidentally, and no insight is given to domestic life, although the host was a woman and appears twice in the book as 'Mistress Catherwood' and listed as 'Marv Catherwood, Victualler' in the local directory. However, the book shows the thoughts, conversation, interests and habits of the seafaring section of the population at an embryonic period in the growth of the port. Many similar convivial gatherings, locally called 'firesides', must have been held in Liverpool and elsewhere during this period, but a detailed record is rare.

This commercial attitude towards the abhorrent trafficking in slavery beggars belief. As shown below, it was also held at the same time by the rural upper-class Mock Corporation of Sefton, a village near Liverpool.

The Prison Doors Should be Thrown Open

Sefton (or Sephton) is a village near Liverpool graced by a fourteenth-century church. The Corporation met on Sundays, coming by gig or carriage, on horseback or on foot. In winter, they met at Bootle Coffee House Bridge, but in more clement weather they enjoyed an early dinner at the Sefton Church Inn (now the Punch Bowl). A sample menu consisted of hare, calf's head and brains, leg of mutton, Yorkshire pudding, potatoes, salad, gooseberry tarts and cheese. Once, this was accompanied by a vintage wine 130 years old. They then attended Sefton Church and might, for fun, time the sermon, 'fifteen minutes and nine seconds and three quarters [of] another second, by three stop-watches held by the umpire which did not vary the one hundred-thousandth part of half a second'.[12] Maybe there was a bet on it.

Afterwards they reassembled at the inn and drank more wine. First, they proposed His Majesty's (George III's) health. On one occasion they expressed that 'General Joy on his Majesty's Happy recovery to health be more generally experienced' and ordered that 'the prison doors be thrown open and persons of all descriptions confined therein, set at liberty' (this did in fact take place). The Lady Patroness was then honoured. She was chosen by a competition in which the members present bid 'so much wine (sometimes many dozens)' for the privilege of nominating the lady. Towards the close of the records (extant from 1771 to 1797) this practice was abandoned as it was deemed rather below the dignity of the Corporation to have their Lady Patroness put up for auction and knocked down to the highest bidder. The nomination was therefore left to the 'Mayor'. After the Lady Patroness, the Corporation then toasted the 'gallant admirals and seamen of the fleets, whose naval victories filled them with unfeigned delight'. The 'Mayor' and other officers were elected, including two 'African Committee men'. In addition, mock titles were conferred on each member as he was admitted. Many of these were whimsical such as Inspector of the Coney Warren, Chafe-wax, Pedestrian Ambassador to the Court of Russia, Butter Weigher, and Brazier and Tinker General.

However, some of them were serious and connected with the slave trade, for example 'Governor of the Tantum Quarry on the Gold Coast', and 'Prince of Anamaboe or Palaver Settler'. In fact, a resolution was unanimously passed in 1788 to send a general petition to the House of Lords protesting against the Bill for restricting the number of slaves to be transported in each ship from Africa to the West Indies and elsewhere. Similarly, the following year, they voted to send up to the House of Commons to show 'the Corporation's indignant sense of the ridiculous motion for abolishing the slave Trade proposed by Fanatic Wilberforce'. Two years later, 'On this day upwards of 200 Sail of Vessels, many of whom had been detained 3 months by contrary 'Winds, in sight & to the great satisfaction of the Burgesses, left the Harbour, to each of whom a successful Voyage was drank, & 3 Cheers given with feelings not to be exprcss'd.' However, most of the time was amicably spent in talking politics or making bets on a favourite horse or cockfighting; listening to accounts of battles in foreign wars or to a strange company of psalm-singers, attended by a band of music. Here they were to be found, to use their own expression, frequently repeated, 'spending the afternoon with the usual festivity, and closing the day with the utmost harmony'.

The Duke of Bridgewater's Canal

Until the end of the seventeenth century, transportation of goods from the Mersey up to Warrington and further up to Manchester was hampered by fish weirs beyond Runcorn. When they were cleared, there still remained the obstacle of mossland before Manchester could be reached. A campaign to construct a canal was joined by Richard Norris of Speke Hall near Liverpool (who traded in slaves, sugar and tobacco). It culminated in the Mersey and Irwell Act of 1721.

However, the usefulness of the canal was limited by its winding course, small locks and low headroom underneath bridges. Boats had then to be hauled by horses or men and this continued towards Manchester, with the towpath changing from side to side. The problem was solved by Francis Egerton, who became the 3rd Duke of Bridgewater in 1748 at the age of 12. When reaching the age of majority, he became engaged to a society beauty in London, but the engagement was broken off and he retired to the family seat at Worsley near Manchester. He was endowed with business acumen and devoted his energies to improving the abysmal communications in the area. These were to be transformed by him and would link Manchester and Liverpool, the two most important towns in the Industrial Revolution. To power this, cheap and readily available energy was needed but supplies of wood were near exhausted and transportation costs for coal were high. The duke owned rich coalfields on his Worsley estate. John Gilbert, the estate manager, suggested a scheme that would drain the mines and create a head of water for a canal to carry the coal to Manchester. When the Mersey and Irwell Navigation objected, a new route was devised that carried the canal by an aqueduct over the River Irwell at Barton. Rubble was used to reclaim boglands such as Trafford Moss. A most effective partnership was formed with John Gilbert as resident engineer, the canal builder James Brindley as consultant and the duke himself steering the project through Parliament.

The Barton Viaduct was built in 1761 to carry the Bridgewater Canal over the River Irwell. Considered one of the seven wonders of the canal age, it was replaced by another wonder of the age, the Barton Swing Bridge, when the Manchester Ship Canal was constructed in 1893. (G.F. Yates)

Following its opening in 1771, the duke proposed an extension that would link up with the River Mersey at Warrington. But once again there was fierce opposition. It would run south of the river (hence in Cheshire), and the Mersey and Irwell Navigation refused permission for their water to be used, but the duke sourced it from his waterlogged mines. Landowners argued that the canal would divide their estates and they would lose land, but they were persuaded that the canal would bring trading benefits to the locality. A plan was put before Parliament to construct a canal from the Potteries to meet the Bridgewater at Preston Brook and then descend to the Mersey at Runcorn. This was linked to the construction of a dock in Liverpool with a double-storeyed warehouse (probably the first in the port, completed in 1783). It would not only receive barges and goods from Manchester and the Potteries but also create an important interchange between those and trade overseas. The network was extended by a canal from Worsley to Leigh that later joined up with the Leeds and Liverpool Canal. It then became a highway for the transportation of cotton, wool, sugar, stone, coal, fish and agricultural produce from Ireland and Wales through to the Midlands. The price of coal in Manchester was halved and the promotion of similar schemes stimulated.

Two months before his death in 1803 the childless duke drew up a will that guaranteed a trust was formed to manage the system and ensure that it would continue to run efficiently. His memorial at Ashridge in Hertfordshire records him as 'Father of Inland Navigation'. His canal certainly has claims to be the first of the modern canals in the world. It was also the forerunner of the Manchester Ship Canal, which brought ocean-going ships into the heart of Manchester. That was an even greater engineering project, admittedly driven by steam instead of muscle power.

Quicker but not Safer

Inland towns reaped enormous benefits from links to the canal system and celebrated the events with matching enthusiasm. When the Leeds and Liverpool Canal reached Blackburn in 1810 it opened up trade across the world, not just to the west via Liverpool but to the east via Leeds and Hull. Twenty-seven vessels with four bands and 7,000 people on board formed the inaugural procession, which was greeted by an estimated 25,000 spectators. At the start of the nineteenth century, the poet Robert Southey praised the comfort and speed of travelling by the Bridgewater Canal at a walking pace of 4mph. You could also choose to pay for seats in parlour or kitchen class and indulge in a dinner equal to that at an inn. Passengers enjoyed conversation ranging from serious political debate to reminiscences while children played around them. However, within four decades these idyllic scenes were ousted by railways, which offered a quicker and cheaper mode of travel. Attempts were made to speed up the canal boats by use of steam engines and an experiment in which a horse plodded around in a circle to turn a paddle wheel. Steam was more successful in transforming travel on open waters from Liverpool, used on a ferry service to Runcorn and on journeys to the end of the Bridgewater Canal at Ellesmere Port. A ship with hybrid propulsion of sail and steam first arrived at Liverpool from America in 1819 after a voyage of twenty-six days. Before the year was out, similar services operated regularly to and from Glasgow, Belfast and Dublin. Within the following decade the coastal towns of Ulverston, Morecambe, Lancaster and Preston were similarly connected, but it was still cheaper to go to Lytham by coach.

Travelling by canal was comparatively safer than other forms of transport. However, incidents were recorded, as in the chaotic celebrations at Blackburn at the opening of the Leeds and Liverpool Canal. Two children and three men fell into the water during the passage but were saved. A man on board who thrust a red hot poker into the mouth of a cannon charged with powder escaped, but with his hand shattered. The unaccustomed and increasing speed and density of traffic on the railways brought its toll but nothing like the risks on the roads. Here, danger was courted by competition between the stagecoaches themselves, and between them and the railways. One of the stagecoaches averaged 14mph between Manchester and Liverpool, twice the speed of the mail coaches. Horses were 'flogged all the way from Bolton'[13] to reach Preston thirty-five minutes before time, to the discomfort of the passengers, and their compassion for the horses. But the worst excesses were committed by the post chaises, light vehicles hired by the wealthy to travel at great speed from one posting inn to another where the horses were changed. Attacks by highwaymen threatened. In one year alone (1830), there were at least three incidents on the road from Liverpool to Manchester. A rider was pulled from his horse by a band of about a dozen men, bound, blindfolded and robbed. The assailants escaped, as they did on another occasion when a marksman's shot passed through a traveller's hat. Three men were arrested in a third attack. The usual penalty was transportation for life.

Businesswoman

Sarah Clayton lived in an age when women were not usually involved in civic and mercantile affairs. However, behind the scenes, she instigated conspicuous achievements that on the pages of history are recorded in the name of men. She was born in 1712 and was 3 years old when her father died. A monument in St Nicholas' Church, Liverpool, records that he had 'being a great incourager of trade and having good judgement in it represented the borough in six distinct parliaments'. In fact, her father had made his fortune as a slave trader and dealer in slave-grown goods. Sarah was on holiday in Bath when she met the architect John Wood and was impressed with him. Hearing that the Corporation had asked him to prepare a plan for the new Exchange (that is, the Town Hall), she wrote a strong letter of recommendation for engaging him to design it. The present Town Hall, although altered after a fire in 1795, stands to this day as a monument to her perspicacity and persuasiveness.

Sarah also inherited an interest as lady of the manor in the Parr Hall estate near St Helens. It contained rich seams of coal but the cost of transporting it was prodigious. It had to be sold in Liverpool at nearly twice the price as at the pithead. In the 1750s she became a member of the committee to survey the turnpike road between Prescot and Ashton and advanced money for its repair. This would engender healthy competition between road and canal to bring down costs and create an alternative route when the canal froze in winter.

Sarah had an interest in the canal as well. She used her own flats (the name given to boats sailing on the Sankey Navigation) to transport the coal mined at Parr Hall and had been instrumental in the construction of the canal in the first place. It had been conceived precisely because of the rising price of transporting coal and Liverpool Corporation (urged on by Sarah?) ordered a survey of the route in 1754. It was decided to cut a canal alongside the Sankey Brook. Although the Bridgewater Canal is usually credited with the accolade of being the first dead-water canal of great length in the country, the Sankey Canal was the first one of any considerable length. Hundreds of navvies, masons, carpenters and carriers worked on it with no mechanical aids. The canal was opened by stages between 1757 and 1759. For the first fifteen years of operation the investors reaped dividends and Sarah appointed a manager (and assistant) to oversee the increasing production of her coal. But the extension of the Bridgewater Canal and then the Leeds and Liverpool took traffic away from the Sankey Navigation.

Sarah's involvement with it has a sad end. Her manager was suspected of mishandling the affairs of her company, which was declared bankrupt a year before her death in her 77th year in 1779. She founded Clayton Square in Liverpool, demolished in 1989, whose replacement still bears her name.

How Much for an Unladen Ass and Cart Drawn by Four Horses, Please?

Two centuries on, a turnpike house still displays its table of tolls at Barrowford. You might like to stop for a moment, imagine what you are bringing past the bar and work out the amount you owe in old money if you bring one from each category! The enforcement of Broad Wheel legislation caused rioting in some areas.

Georgian Innovation and Change

The Toll House at Barrowford, dating from the early nineteenth century, has now been converted into a modern home. Note the Georgian features with framed doorway and sash windows.

The Marston-Long Preston Turnpike Trust

A Table of the Tolls To Be Taken At Barrowford Bar

HORSES & CATTLE	For Every Horse or Ass, Laden or Unladen and not drawing	the sum of	0s 1d
	For every Score of Oxen or Cattle, Calves, Sheep or Swine	the sum of	0s 10d
COACHES & CHAISES	For Every Coach drawn by six Horses	the sum of	3s 0d
	Chaise one Horse		0s 6d
	For Every Waggon having Wheels Of Less Breadth than Six Inches and drawn by Six Horses	the sum of	3s 0d
WAGGONS	For Every Six Inch Wheeled Waggon Nine		
	drawn by fewer than Four Horses		1s 0d
	Eight	the sum of	2s 0d
CARTS	For every Cart Having Wheels of less Breadth than Six Inches and drawn by Three Horses	the sum of	1s 6d
	For Every Six Inch Wheeled Cart, drawn Nine		1s 4d
	By Four Horses	the sum of	1s 0d

THE ABOVE TOLL CHARGES ARE TO BE TAKEN FOR THE FIRST & EVERY FIFTH TIME OF PASSING THRO EACH BAR

BY ORDER

Turnpikes were late coming to Lancashire. They were the best roads since Roman times. Tracks from the Dark Ages and Medieval times were damaged by the increasing volume and weight of heavy goods wagons carrying coal, timber and stone besides agricultural produce. They were filled with ruts as much as 4ft deep and rendered impassable through flooding. Although this was a hindrance to travel in a burgeoning industrial age, it was not until 1724 that an act was passed for a Lancashire turnpike, sixty years after the first in the country. Lancashire was still a backwater, socially, politically and economically, due in no small measure to its remote location from the capital. The tiring and uncomfortable journey to London could take a week for a horseman and up to two weeks for a coach. Danger threatened from highwaymen and accidents.

A turnpike (by derivation) was a stretch of road protected by a bar that had to be turned (and a toll paid!) for traffic to proceed. A trust was created, usually by local businessmen, landowners, farmers or professional people, to take responsibility for a section of road. The income could be used for maintenance and payment of interest on loans. At first the roads were simply upgraded but from the 1820s new roads were built on a different alignment with substantial engineering work. Some of these retain their original line and can be identified today by 'new road', as in Preston, Blackburn, Bolton and Ashton in Manchester. To aid economic expansion, an infrastructure of turnpike roads was extended from 1750 onwards until 1842, when the last one in Lancashire was completed from Chorley to Blackburn. The county network then totalled 750 miles but the trusts were wound up in the 1870s and '80s and the last one handed over to Lancashire County Council in 1890.

By then they had improved travelling schedules remarkably, cutting the journey time by coach to London down to a week. In 1825 a Royal Union coach would leave for Liverpool from one of the four coaching inns in Blackburn every Thursday and Friday at 4.30 a.m., presumably to ensure arrival at a reasonable time that day. But the pace of change accelerated. In 1838, soon after the Liverpool & Manchester Railway opened, there were still ten coach offices in Liverpool, but the railway network was growing apace. Mail was received by rail from many of the largest towns in the country, although a mail coach (for which passengers paid a premium fare) ran to Lancaster.

A COLLIERY GIRL'S WIGANSPEAK

In the Georgian and Victorian ages millions of tracts were printed and distributed in leaflet form. Their aim was to preach about the social evils and virtues of the times based on moral or religious principles. Often, they would be put in a narrative form, describing the imaginary life of someone beset by hardship and winning against all odds with the help of a benefactor (like Sissy in Charles Dicken's novel *Hard Times*, based in Preston). The philanthropist and religious writer Hannah More wrote a tract based on an article in the *Gentleman's Magazine* of 1795. Rarely can a name be attached to a real person and the reality proved by research in registers and personal encounter but such a one is Betty Harwood. Betty, aged 9, and her brother, aged 7, were working in a coal mine near Upholland with their father when he was killed by a stone falling down the mine shaft. Her mother became mentally deranged in her grief. By means of working a double shift (probably fifteen hours a day), she was able to bring her mother and two brothers out of the workhouse into a cottage. They died, she fell ill and had to leave the colliery to seek less onerous work. The local squire found employment for her in his household, and she grew up to be promoted to cook. She was left £50 in his will, over four times her salary for the year. A friend of the squire tracked Betty down and was attracted by her appearance, honesty and good sense. She had the ability to express herself clearly, confidently and concisely. He even recorded her Wigan accent: 'When th'French doa cum, if weemen ma feight, I'll feight as ard as I con.' (When the French do come, if women may fight, I'll fight as hard as I can). She persuaded her brother to enlist: 'Go wi the nebor lads, theyle caw thee keweart' (Go with the local [neighbour] lads, or they'll call you a coward) and 'tha know, lad, work's neaw a das skearse' (you know, lad, work's nowadays scarce).

NOTHING EXCEPT A SUP OF COLD WATER

Conditions in the mines were incredibly terrifying. According to one observer, the best mine was more demoralising than the worst factory. One girl born in 1812 was just under 7 when her father carried her down a series of fifteen ladders on his back into the pit. He might have had to pay for his own candles to warn him of danger. If the flame spurted up the gas would be about to fire. The safety lamp was invented in 1814 but it was not in common use for years afterwards. Most likely, the girl would eventually be at work for up to twelve hours a day 'with nothing except a sup of cold water'. She could be on her hands and feet with a belt about her waist and a chain between her legs drawing tubs of coal from the coal face to where the ponies could take over. One girl gave birth down the mine the day after she married and was beaten by her 'feller' (husband) if she was not ready in time.

The workers rarely washed and were often completely drenched all day long underground, anyway. The youngest children were employed to open and close the air doors for the waggoners to pass, akin to a pitiable and monotonous solitary confinement. A boy of 9, put in charge of the steam-operated winding gear, turned away to look at a mouse. He failed to stop the cage coming up the shaft and the four miners inside were carried over the beam, tipped down the shaft and killed. Punishment could be so severe that boys were rendered incapable of work. Local rules stipulated that all miners should 'attend divine service at least once on the Lord's Day' and forbade the men to begin work on a Monday morning dirty or with an old beard.

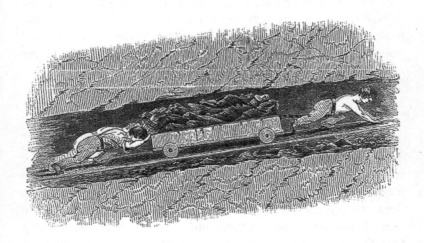

Children in the mines working the belt and chain system of drawing baskets and tubs used in the early 1800s.

A Plump for an Improper Touch

Thanks to the pressure on public opinion exerted by tract writers and others, working conditions were improved and an act of 1842 forbade women from going down the pit, although it was allowed on the surface. But it was often deliberately ignored, and ladders were secretly provided to enable them to continue employment. Victorian sexual morality intervened with mixed results. The practice, shocking to many elsewhere in the country, was prevalent in Lancashire, where over a thousand women hauled coal along at the pit face, particularly in the Wigan area. There, it was common and a convention for pregnant women to accompany their husbands, and if a male touched a girl improperly her brother would 'plump' him. For a few years after 1842 women were smuggled underground by husbands or brothers, which prompted calls to the police. There were attempts by diehard 'male only' miners to exclude women even on the top, until the First World War liberated them. Maybe they were helped by parading in London wearing their working suits: decent trousers. Although it was argued that a father would look after his children well and they would give a much-needed boost to the family income, it was decreed that no child should be employed underground.

An International Reputation

There were exceptions to the general rule of indifference to the treatment of coal miners. The Countess of Ellesmere, whose husband had inherited the Bridgewater estates, opened a domestic science school for the displaced women and girls, the first of its kind in the country, and the earl obliged mine boys to attend day schools and evening technical classes, where a qualified teacher instructed them in ventilation, machinery and gases. A few years later, in 1847, the baton was handed on to the Wigan Technical and Mining School, the second oldest in the country after the Royal School of Mines. One master and about fifty students met in a public hall for classes in mining, geology, chemistry and mechanics. In 1883 the school moved into more spacious accommodation facing the library for over a hundred students. The temporary building, a 'tin tabernacle', more often used for emergent churches, provided lecture halls, a laboratory and model room, all heated by hot water. Collections of fossils, minerals and geological maps were donated, and students won first, second and fifth places in the national honours awards. It had gained an international reputation.

ALL THIS WE ENDURE FOR THE GOOD OF THE COUNTRY AT LARGE

If anything, the miners had more grievances than their textile companions but did not resort to violence as they did. Admittedly, they were not put out of work by new technology but their working conditions were atrocious. At first coalminers expressed their dissatisfaction in conciliatory terms. A handbill urging miners to attend a meeting on Kersal Moor in 1818 'announces to the public' that they are asking for consideration of working hours shorter than twelve hours a day in dangerous conditions: 'we are in danger of our lives every moment, and all this we endure for the good of the country at large'. How true! Ironically, the second golf course in the land was founded on Kersal Moor by a group of Manchester businessmen that same year. Twenty years later, it would be a favourite venue for meetings of the political activists, the Chartists, at one time amassing a crowd of some 50,000.

A colliers 'strike' of 1881 was in fact a lock out and the catalyst for it the passing of the Employers Liability Act. This made the employers liable to pay compensation to their workers or their families if they were negligent. In Wigan at the time two-thirds of patients in the infirmary were mine workers and the act aimed to encourage employers to improve safety in the mines. But, fearing that they would have to pay for safety improvements, they opted out of the act and gave their employees an ultimatum: either join a relief society that gave them no protection against negligence or lose their jobs. Many refused and were joined by others campaigning for reinstatement of wage reductions and for payment weekly rather than fortnightly. The dispute lasted seven weeks. Protest meetings of tens of thousands of workers were planned. The Home Office advised that it was illegal to prohibit the gatherings. Instead, magistrates announced they would ban musical bands and prosecute anyone who obstructed roads. They also expanded local police forces, augmented by the military. A rapid response system included two trains permanently in steam to rush forces to flash points, one of them involving a meeting held by women. Such intimidating moves and conciliatory behaviour by the workers ensured that there was only one serious incident, which involved stone throwing against strike breakers as the miners gradually resumed work.

So Long to Our Cursed Landlord

Lancashire lost much of its talent to emigration in the Georgian period and beyond. Captain Standish from Duxbury (both Lancashire place names) sailed with the Pilgrim Fathers on the *Mayflower* in 1620. Factors included religion (Puritans, Quakers and Mormons, for example) or sheer desperation to gain a better life combined with a sense of adventure. David Cragg was one, but most of all for another reason as it turned out. He sprang from typical Lancashire yeoman farmer stock in Wyresdale, attested from at least the seventeenth century by initials on farm buildings. David kept a diary giving a vivid account of the family's dairy farming. The highlight was a visit to the Lancaster cheese fair in October, setting off before dawn and bartering until dusk. He had four brothers and three sisters. The land could not support so many, as we shall see. His first married home was only two up and two down (the parlour and the buttery). The main fuel was turf or peat. When this ran out, coal had to be fetched from a distance along poor roads. Aged 11, he was taught to read and write at a local chapel along with his sister. Later, he built up a little library of books that he bought at Preston and Lancaster markets. He was a member of the Society of Friends, the Quakers, as were many of his neighbours, but suffered from the depredations of the chief landowner. His wife converted to be a Quaker to marry him, and eight children were born to them before she died. His cousin and brother had already emigrated to America when he too decided to sail from Wyresdale to join them. He noted in his diary as he left, 'So long William and all the tithes, taxes, church rates, parsons and parasites ... and our cursed landlord.' The family wrote home with news of the plenty of work and good wages, as their relatives must have done before them, and so emigration escalated.

7

THE WORLD'S FIRST INDUSTRIAL REVOLUTION

From Cottage to Factory

Britain was the first industrial nation and Lancashire cotton its first highly developed industry. In the late Medieval period, wool from sheep farming was sold by chapmen peddling their wares from village to village. The eighteenth century witnessed a cottage industry with women and children engaged on preparation work while the men worked the looms with textiles of fustians and calico. When water and muscle power was replaced by coal and steam, huge factories sprang up with hundreds of workers, men on the heavier machines and women and children on the lighter duties. New technology started the process in the 1760s, when Hargreave's spinning jenny increased the rate of production of yarn per person by 100 per cent. This was followed in 1769 by Richard Arkwright's water frame, which replaced the power of the hand with the watermill and then steam. This had to be utilised at a central point away from the cottages, which led more than anything else to the development of the factory system. A decade later, Crompton's mule produced mechanical spinning so fine that muslin could be manufactured, although it required great skill, strength and dexterity. Advances were made in weaving, too. John Kay's fly shuttle had been patented in 1733 but there had been so much opposition to his invention that he took refuge in France. However, home production was stimulated by Arkwright's carding engine of 1775, Cartwright's power loom of 1787 and the French Revolution. In 1793 weavers were so prosperous that they could travel to work in a coach. Despite improvements by William Horrocks in 1802, ten years later there were still only 2,400 power looms in Britain and the number of handloom weavers kept rising to a peak of 250,000 in 1825. In Blackburn, most of the weaving was still being carried out in cottages: 'putter-outs' acted as middlemen who distributed cotton yarn to handloom weavers and then sold their products on the market. Some cloth was woven in weavers' sheds to avoid transportation of goods to and fro between places of work. There were numerous family-controlled firms with local and personal networking. Cottages were built specially for the purpose with triple windows to shed light onto cellar loomshops.

A Clever Mule

Samuel Crompton, a key figure in the Industrial Revolution, was born on a farm near Bolton in 1753. The building still survives as part of a typical Lancashire hamlet of the time with houses grouped around a central courtyard. Samuel's father died when he was aged 5 but he received a good education until he was 16, unusual for the time, and worked with textiles in the family business. Inheriting an inventive streak from his father, who had helped to build an organ gallery and organ, he turned his mind to improving the manufacturing process.

At the age of 26 he eventually devised his mule, so called as it was the combination of two distinct processes: the spinning jenny that had been invented by Hargreaves about 1764 and the waterwheel by Arkwright in 1775. Crompton's mule improved the quality and quantity of the thread and muslins. However, by nature secretive and unsociable, he was afraid of the antagonism already evinced in riots and loom breaking, so he kept his invention hidden in an attic entered by a trap door. The local textile fraternity were keen to discover the process and spied on him. It is said that Arkwright paid him a visit but, as luck would have it, Crompton was out when he called. Otherwise, if they had met, there could have been a winning partnership as Arkwright was a shrewd businessman. As it was, Crompton was inveigled into giving away his prototype machine, which was copied by others, for a paltry sum. However, he rectified his mistake by refining his invention and patenting that. Three times he refused a partnership in a local firm run by Robert Peel, father of the future Prime Minister, but he was able to invest money raised through a public subscription to maintain a thriving business.

His invention had meanwhile attracted national attention and Crompton travelled to Parliament in 1812 hoping for government recognition for the profit to the economy that his invention had brought. He was supported by Sir Robert Peel (Robert's son, later Prime Minister) and Lord Stanley (13th Earl of Derby). It seems that in the House of Parliament lobby he overheard Spencer Percival, the Prime Minister, mentioning an award of as much as £20,000 (well over £1 million today). Moments later, luck deserted Samuel again. Percival was assassinated and a committee chaired by Lord Stanley awarded Crompton only £5,000. Public subscriptions were needed to save him from further deteriorating business ventures, secure him an annuity and pay for a memorial to him thirty-five years after his death in 1827.

SMASH THE LOOMS!

Working people slowly formed associations to press for better conditions, which the government resisted by Combination Acts and the Riot Act. By the mid-1820s handloom weavers and their dependents constituted about 60 per cent of the population of east Lancashire. During the economic depression at the start of the nineteenth century, the government failed to support starving weavers, who organised themselves to march under the

Luddites smashing looms.

banner of the legendary General Ludd, directed by 'captains'. In a series of disturbances in 1812, ten rioters were killed in Middleton, many more wounded and eight hanged later in Lancashire as ringleaders. The handloom weavers' sole target in the uprising was the destruction of power looms in cotton mills. It drew political attention and much-needed financial assistance to the desperate plight of the weavers' communities. The government was so alarmed that it sent more troops to quell the disturbances than to Spain to fight Napoleon. The Law Breaking Act was passed carrying the death penalty. Lord Byron protested, 'As the sword is the worst argument that can be used, so should it be the last.'

Greater Hardship than Slavery

Life in the factories had its own cruelties, even barbarities. The incessant rhythm and increasing speed of the waterwheel and steam engine had a dehumanising effect on the operatives. Numerous factories allowed no time for breakfast, which workers ate off the floor or on a makeshift shelf nailed over the pulley. Half-naked and reeking with perspiration, they would race from one machine to another desperately trying to keep up with the inhuman monster that might spew out a shuttle into their eye. Larger and faster machines reduced the workforce but increased the dangers and the efforts of the individual. Adults were subjected to arbitrary rules and fines for breaking them. This included, for example, the whole department being liable for double the fine if the perpetrator could not be identified. It was said that one master advanced his clock during the night and fined the workers for turning up late in the morning. Sitting, talking, whistling or singing could be penalised. A newspaper commented that the workers endured 'much greater hardship than negro slaves'. Working hours in the mills were harsh, often operating twelve hours a day, Monday to Friday, and nine hours on a Saturday.

Women, who outnumbered men, were particularly hard pressed. Forced to work to feed their family and unable to afford a child minder, they resorted to opium or other drugs to keep their children quiet. They were unable to breastfeed their children while at work, expressing their milk and throwing it away. Their physical and mental health deteriorated.

Children as young as 6 might work a day shift of twelve hours with only one and a half hours for meals or a corresponding night shift: 'the beds *never* got cold'. Boys would enter mills as half timers, maybe unpaid, helping to oil and clean the looms so that a mother or sister could work an extra machine to bring more money into the family. They were particularly useful as their size enabled them to get underneath the machines and their small fingers were ideal for tying fine broken threads. Accidents would occur when children cleaned the floor under machines at work or carried out maintenance work during meal breaks or at the end of the day. They might be forced to stand the whole time and Sunday mornings were spent cleaning the machinery. Discipline was enforced by brutal corporal punishment akin to torture. Children would fall asleep on the factory floor, run away, contemplate suicide or even be dumped elsewhere to make their own way back to parishes for help when the factory owner went bankrupt. They might endure cold and wet on a 4-mile tramp from home to the mill and back. The suffering that such physical hardships engendered could last them for adult life, or shorten it, if they survived that long. Children under 9 were eventually forbidden from working, although some parents regretted the loss of income. In 1830 a hand loom weaver was arrested for employing children who led a life akin to slave labour. They worked from 5 a.m. one day to 2 a.m. the following day, were not allowed out of the house and were fed on porridge, or occasionally potatoes. Unsatisfactory work was punished by a beating with a knotted rope or reduction to one meal a day.

As the workers were paid piece time, they would do anything to maintain production even when an accident occurred and a machine was being repaired. Faster machines meant more flying needles and lost eyes. Everyone was affected by the artificial steaming of the atmosphere to reduce the breakages of the thread but in the dressing room they would work at 105°F (41°C), above the permitted 80°–95°F to increase their output.

In 1832 a Bill was presented to Parliament to limit the daily working hours of children under 18 years of age to ten (!). Banners with slogans were carried through Manchester in support. One depicted a deformed operative with the plaint 'Am I not a man and a brother?' Another was borne by factory children. One of them, holding an overseer's whip and a strap made into thongs, pleaded 'Behold and weep'. The turning point in working conditions came with the passing of the Ten Hours

Act of 1848 and a paid inspectorate to enforce it. Even then, in 1858 Sarah Parker Remond, an American abolitionist, declared in a speaking tour in Britain, 'When I walk through the streets of Manchester and meet load after load of cotton, I think of those 80,000 cotton plantations on which was grown the $125 million worth of cotton which supply your market and I remember that not 1 cent of that money has ever reached the hands of the labourers.' $125 million would be worth nearly £5 billion today. Parker Remond added, 'England's bread hangs by Lancashire's thread.' Did she inspire 'The Ragged-Trousered Philanthropists'?

A Tragedy Performed in Three Scenes

Scene 1: Monday, 16 August 1819, St Peter's Field in Manchester.

The 'Field' is a piece of waste ground that is being cleared for redevelopment in the centre of Manchester. It is completely surrounded by buildings or walls except for the streets that lead off it.

Characters:
- A huge crowd estimated at 50,000 from all over south-west Lancashire, including women and the elderly. They want reform of the electoral system that deprives Manchester of a Member of Parliament.
- Samuel Bamford, a weaver poet, who has been arrested three years before on a march to London to ask for electoral reform. The group have been christened the 'Blanketeers' because they each carried a blanket to keep themselves warm at night.
- Henry 'Orator' Hunt has spoken at mass meetings in London urging Parliamentary reform and has been invited to speak at this one. The address that he printed for the meeting has exhorted them to come 'with no other weapon but that of a self-approving conscience'. He advocates annual elections and votes for all, including women.

- Revd W.R. Hay: a notoriously biased magistrate. Four years earlier he had sent thirty-seven reformers arrested at a meeting to go for trial at Lancaster. The case against them was dismissed.
- William Hulton: Chairman of Magistrates.
- Two cavalry regiments: the Hussars and the Yeomanry Cavalry.

The crowd gathers. It is a hot summer's day and many are in their Sunday best clothes. Some enter, marching in an orderly fashion. They have been drilled to do so, but others interpret this as being part of a rebel military operation. None are armed. They fill the field until they are packed 'hat to hat'. William Hulton is looking across St Peter's Field from the magistrates' house to the hustings where Henry Hunt is going to address the multitude. Revd Hay tries (not too hard) to read the Riot Act, which should encourage the crowd to disperse and warn them of the consequences if they don't. William is alarmed by the huge crowd and sends a message to the commanders of the two cavalry regiments, who are on standby in case of trouble, that they should 'preserve the peace'. The Yeomanry are the first to arrive and charge through the crowd. Such is their haste that one of them knocks a 2-year-old child from his mother's arms. He is killed, the first casualty of the 'massacre'. Henry Hunt is arrested but the troopers become separated from each other. They panic and slash at the specially made banners and flags, then indiscriminately amongst the crowd. The Hussars arrive and are ordered to disperse the meeting. Even though they use only the flats of their swords, many are crushed underfoot as the crowd flees and tries to force a way through the limited and narrow exits. In ten minutes the field is deserted except for the debris of torn clothing and discarded hats and shoes. At least eleven lie dead and 600 wounded. More will die from their injuries. In the illustration (opposite), the Hussars (top left) are yelling 'Down with 'em!', etc., as in the caption. The banner is headed 'LOYAL MANCHESTER YEOMANRY' and continues 'So Bloody Bold and Resolute'.

The World's First Industrial Revolution

'Down with 'em! Chop 'em down my brave boys – give them no quarter. They want to take our Beef and Pudding from us and remember the more you kill the less poor rates you'll have to pay so go at it Lads show your courage and your Loyalty.'

Scene 2: The Houses of Parliament, London.

Characters:
- Duke of Wellington (Prime Minister).
- The Cabinet.

There is discussion on how to act following nationwide condemnation of what is immediately dubbed a massacre. The Cabinet is worried that if they do not back those in authority there may be a breakdown of law and order, even a revolution like the one in France that precipitated the Napoleonic War (concluded only four years earlier). It is decided that no action or prosecution is to be taken against those in authority.

Scene 3: A magistrates' court at different places on different occasions.

Characters:
- Hunt
- Bamford
- Revd Hay

Hunt is sentenced to eighteen months' imprisonment.

Bamford and three others are sentenced to a year's imprisonment. (Bamford later wrote about his life as a radical activist with an eyewitness account of the treatment of the Luddites in Middleton. He is honoured with an obelisk in Middleton Cemetery, where he is buried, and a garden and plaque where his former house stood.)

Revd Hay is removed to a distant parish.

None of the assailants received any reprimand or punishment. The massacre at St Peter's Field was immediately called 'Peterloo' as the Hussars had taken part in the Battle of Waterloo (won by Wellington only four years before). Unfortunately, Manchester's greatest day only led in the short term to severe repression of any organised gatherings on the path to reform. But it was a turning point in British history. Lancashire working people were elevated in their own eyes and in the opinion of the middle class. However, the government passed the notorious six acts to stem agitation, and it was not until the Reform Act of 1832 that Manchester was able to elect a Member of Parliament and women had to wait another hundred years for the vote.

LAKE DISTRICT DISCONTENT

William Wordsworth was a pupil from 1779, aged 9, until 1787 at the grammar school in Hawkshead, the most northerly village in Lancashire. In his poem 'The Prelude', Wordsworth describes his school time there: 'What happiness to live/When every hour brings palpable access/Of knowledge, when all knowledge is delight/And sorrow is not there!' His was an idyllic boyhood before the Industrial Revolution changed the landscape, and the towns of South Lancashire were wracked by the strains of cotton manufacturing. But the countryside of North Lancashire over the sands of Morecambe Bay did have its own troubles.

The dalesmen of High Furness were particularly dependent on employment in the slate quarries and mines. About the year 1800, peaceful protests led to open revolt with unbelievable consequences. In the midst of the Napoleonic War, bad harvests afflicted the country with famine. The price of wheat doubled in a year and the price of oatmeal, their staple diet, quadrupled. Every other source of food became exhausted. Even the nettles at the side of the road disappeared. The dalesmen heard that the dearth of oatmeal was due to the millers of Ulverston withholding their stocks in the hope of prices rising when they would harvest an increased profit. They decided to march on the town, gathering strength on their way like a snowball and finding welcome sustenance on dried beans in a deserted mill. They persuaded another miller to sell his produce in the marketplace the next day and he rewarded them for their good conduct with money to buy drinks at the pub. On reaching Ulverston, they discovered a large quantity of flour and oatmeal hidden in a warehouse under straw, which they loaded onto handcarts and took to the marketplace. There, they offered it free to anyone who came. When the stocks were rapidly reduced by the crowds who arrived to benefit from this unprecedented circumstance, the mill owners were forced to agree to the sale of their stores on the next three market days. The rioters dispersed and amazingly no action was taken against them. They were all in it together so no ringleaders could be identified; they had the sympathy of the magistrates; and they had not committed damage to any property or violence on any person.

A year or two later another grievance arose. During wartime conditions, a recurring ballot was held to draft the people into military service. Men were forced to leave their homes and many were never seen again. Emboldened by their previous success, the dalesmen decided to descend on Ulverston again at a time when the magistrates had met to conduct the ballot. The rioters invaded the meeting and ordered the officials to leave. Only one refused and he followed soon after, having been suspended out of the window by his feet. All the papers were burnt and, mission accomplished, the rioters returned home. This time the authorities could not allow the disturbance to be overlooked. The military were summoned to hunt the perpetrators down. However, an efficient advance warning system enabled the suspects to escape into the wildness of the fells. Some sought employment elsewhere; others volunteered to enlist(!); and a remnant surrendered and were put on trial at Lancaster but were released on payment of costs.

So ended an episode that demonstrates the independence of the inhabitants in the far north of the Historic County.

Riots

In 1826 a severe trade depression provoked power loom riots. In parts of Lancashire 60 per cent of weavers were out of work, and those who were in employment were paid only a twelfth of what they had earned a generation before, and that by working sixteen hours a day. From this they could afford just one meal a day of oats and water. Butchers and publicans could no longer maintain their trade. The government and manufacturers were deaf to their pleas. The only solution was to destroy the power looms. A body of 6,000 loom wreckers descended on Blackburn armed with sharpened iron fixed to staves, scythes, sledgehammers and a few guns and pistols. The Riot Act was read repeatedly and 237 looms were destroyed in spite of attempts by the military to stop them. Ten thousand rioters paraded through the town boasting that not a single power loom remained unbroken. Throughout the county, in the space of three days, twenty-one mills were attacked and more than a thousand power looms destroyed. One group, opposed by a troop of horse soldiers, protested, 'Are we to starve to death?' The soldiers opened their haversacks and spread their sandwiches among the crowd.

However, on another occasion, the Riot Act was read at Chatterton to a mob of nearly 3,000, who pelted the military with stones. Six hundred bullets were fired into the crowd and six people died on the spot. The number who died later of their wounds remains unclear; a seventh protester died later due to a 'visitation of God' (a heart attack) brought on after receiving a death sentence. A large number of special constables were hired, who arrested twenty ring leaders in the dead of night. Their followers were so frightened that they would not go to sleep in their own houses, and many left the country. There was no public access to the Chatterton inquests. Despite claims that soldiers opened fire because they feared for their lives in the face of a violent crowd, no protesters were prosecuted. The Rifle Corps was quickly redeployed to Portugal. Forty-one people involved in the uprising received the death penalty. All but ten had their sentences commuted to imprisonment, but the remaining protesters, including Mary Hindle, who had merely been an observer, were transported to Australia. Mary took her own life some years later, in despair at the loss of her family and the hope of ever returning to Lancashire. Shamefully and tragically, when charitable financial support from London was allocated to the weavers, much of it was surreptitiously acquired by the mill owners to replace their destroyed power looms. Many hundreds died of starvation after the uprising, including 137 children under the age of 4 who died in nearby Haslingden the following year.

In conciliation, some of the manufacturers agreed on a standard wage and appealed to William Huskisson, then President of the Board of Trade, to legislate a minimum wage. He refused on the grounds that it would prevent freedom of bargaining between labourer and employer. The weavers' distress grew worse. Many were near starvation and in one area half of them were without bedding or clothes.

Hardships and Improvements in Workhouses

In difficult times the workhouse alleviated distress but the provision was criticised by reformers. Joseph Livesey of Preston argued that it would be far better to keep families together at home and administer the aid there. It was also considered a degrading prison by its inmates and some people in authority aimed to make it so. Men, women and children were separated and at times there was appalling overcrowding. Disease was rife and a fever ward might be constructed only after much argument and delay. Charitable sermons and subscriptions raised money for relief and 'paupers' were employed on public works, especially roads (on one occasion under the supervision

An illustration from a newspaper of people queuing for food and coal tickets at a District Provident Society office in Manchester during the cotton famine.

of John McAdam, inventor of the road surface). In 1843 soup kitchens were provided. Later, oatmeal was distributed but then discontinued because of the cost and lack of money. In 1834 the Poor Law Act was passed to set up unions to alleviate the distress of the populace following the economic downturn after the Napoleonic Wars.

Leigh (near Wigan) set up its Union Board soon after. This is an indication of the severity of unemployment at the time and also the desire of the better off to do their duty and help paupers.

The Boards of Guardians were caught between the demands of the ratepayers to keep the rates down and at the same time to make the life of the inmates tolerable and worthwhile. The records of the Leigh Union Board from 1837 to 1848 show how this developed. A major consideration was to find suitable accommodation. At first this was makeshift, with three to a bed –two adults and one child. Then a purpose-built workhouse was constructed. People were most reluctant to enter the workhouse as their freedom was restricted and families might be fragmented by the male–female divide, so they attempted to escape. Every effort was made to generate income and thus reduce costs. A vegetable garden grew vegetables and potatoes for home consumption and a smithy manufactured nails for sale. Children were chosen to go into service or to help women silk weavers. The paupers helped farmers with scything and grinding corn. Finally, they were set to work breaking stones and picking old ropes to extract and recycle oakum (a tarry material used to seal gaps in building ships). A smart drub cord uniform was designed for men and boys, like those of railway porters with a pocket in the jacket and lined trousers. The paupers wore clogs (but the schoolmaster was provided with shoes). When smallpox broke out, the governors set up vaccination centres, and they distributed 5,000 handbills in a cholera outbreak to educate the public and prevent the disease. Staffing was a difficulty. Local people registered complaints about surgeons, the governor's handling of the financial books and the disposal of cotton fabrics. A legal battle developed with the vicar who, illegally, refused to baptise or bury paupers, although, whatever their religion, they were obliged to attend the churches that the Guardians chose. A schoolmaster was employed half-time and his work impressed the inspectorate but because of the severe poverty at the time, his pay was cut to £5 a year, a quarter of the original agreement.

In Wigan, the hopes of the 1834 Act took time and goodwill to materialise. In Bolton, it involved a scandal in 1842 to unearth horrific failings, and then improvement. In one workhouse, consisting of thirteen cottages, 300 paupers slept in 119 beds with families sharing a bed and single beds reserved for fever patients. Children under 10 went to infant school, the older ones attended Sunday school. Most adults picked oakum or were engaged on household jobs. A curfew at 7 p.m. was enforced. Inmates were not allowed to attend Sunday church services as they took the opportunity to drink themselves disorderly. Then came a series of incidents that raised public awareness and alarm. A woman died 'from want of food'. A 73-year-old who had been ill for a year and became 'bedfast' was half-suffocated by a drunken nurse, pronounced dead, prepared for burial, found to be alive but died later. The nurse was not sacked, which provoked a strike among the other occupants. Failure to cut hair had led to an infestation of lice. The Tories on the Board of Governors blamed a radical plot but an inquiry uncovered the scourges of scarlet fever, 'bad eyes' and consumption. However, a new purpose-built workhouse was eventually constructed, which was well staffed with chaplain, teachers and administrative staff. It was self-sufficient with its own chapel and useful occupations were taught on site.

The World's First Inter-City Railway

Cotton, canals and coal triggered industrial change in Lancashire. The railways fired it into a revolution. Coal powered the locomotives that transported coal efficiently to create power wherever it was needed and then distribute the manufactured goods. The greatest impetus was given by the Liverpool & Manchester Railway, the first inter-city railway in the world. It was the means of more efficient transportation of freight between the two centres of manufactured goods (Manchester) and supplying and distributing raw materials and products (Liverpool) Carrying passengers was initially of less importance. In addition, the winner of a trial to select the most reliable locomotive was of a revolutionary design. Not only did it increase the tractive power for the existing system but it stayed as the standard pattern for the following century and a half. The engineering of the line raised standards, too: its monumental engineering triumphs are intact and capable of supporting the present generation of 100mph trains.

The idea of the railway emerged as the answer to an urgent need to improve communications between the two largest and growing conurbations in the county to the benefit of both. A company, twelve directors from each town, was formed in 1824. George Stephenson, with his previous experience on the Stockton & Darlington Railway, was appointed to manage the project. Surveying began, which was met by vehement opposition, especially from landowners, canal companies and investors in turnpikes. Violence broke out. The company launched a vigorous publicity campaign in preparation for presenting a Bill to Parliament. Ironically, as it turned out, one of the principal backers was the Liverpool MP and President of the Board of Trade, William Huskisson. However, there were local heavyweight opponents, including Lord Derby and Lord Sefton. Stephenson was cross-examined in numerous committee meetings and suffered humiliation from clever lawyers, who exploited his naivete and lack of linguistic agility. Scorn was poured on plans to float the railway 5 miles over the fathomless bog of Chat Moss. The Bill was lost, but Stephenson was determined to fight on against the manifest ignorance and lack of foresight exhibited by his adversaries. Learning from their mistakes, the promoters returned to battle and ensured that the bill was passed a year later.

Formidable obstacles had to be overcome on the ground. The seemingly impossible track over Chat Moss was just one that had to be solved simultaneously with others. Rubble sank into the mud, and men were terrified by the prospect of falling in. Many narrowly escaped asphyxiation. Stephenson used a brushwood base to complete a firm track. The Roby Embankment, 3 miles long and 45ft high, the Olive Mount cutting, 2 miles long and up to 100ft deep, and the Sankey railway viaduct (the world's oldest) of nine arches, 50ft wide and 70ft high, ensured that the track was virtually level throughout. A mini-marvel is a skew bridge carrying a turnpike road over the railway at Rainhill. All still stand to this day, creating a line that conveys trains far bigger and faster than could have been imagined. In addition, at the Liverpool end, two tunnels were bored, one of 290 yards to the passenger terminus at Crown Street, and the other 2,250 yards (a mile and a quarter) to the all-important goods terminus at Wapping Dock.

Huskisson was one of 3,000 people who walked throughout its great length on one open day. Traffic through the inclined tunnels to the termini at the Liverpool end was to be rope hauled, powered by stationary steam engines. It had originally been envisaged that these would also operate the rest of the line, but at a late stage steam locomotives, as built by Stephenson for the recently opened Stockton & Darlington Railway, came into consideration. A competition was then organised on level track at Rainhill to ascertain whether traction by a locomotive would be better than a stationary engine. Four locomotives challenged for the prize at these Rainhill Trials in 1829. *Novelty*, the first to appear in the demonstration run, was well named and a pretty sight with its blue livery and highly polished copper cylinders. A railed platform enclosed an upright boiler and tall, thin chimney. It was credited with a speed of over 20mph in advance publicity runs, but on the day it stopped with a display of fireworks caused by the steam pressure rupturing the bellows that forced the draught through the furnace. Next came the *Sans Pareil* with horizontal boiler, attached sturdy chimney and coupled wheels, but it failed two of the conditions set for entry: the machine was overweight and not fitted with springs. Anyway, the boiler was faulty, the exhaust emitted burning cinders and the coke consumption was too high. The *Perseverance*, akin to the *Novelty* in appearance, managed only 6mph over a short distance, failing the rules on both counts. *Rocket*, built by George and Robert Stephenson and like the *Sans Pareil* in design, added a truly revolutionary feature: the multi-tube boiler. This produced extra steam and the familiar chuffing sound we still enjoy as the exhaust from the cylinders drew the heat from the firebox as it passed through the chimney. *Rocket* hauled a load of 13 tons at nearly 30mph, twenty times over a distance of 1½ miles, satisfying all the conditions and far exceeding some.

A Disastrous Celebration

The stage was set for a grand opening in 1830. In the meantime, a huge gateway had been built at Edge Hill at the entrance to the tunnels. It was designed in the shape of a beautiful Moorish arch, and called so, but the towers on each side housed the steam engines to power the rope haulage system. Seven further locomotives of the same design as *Rocket* had been built to haul a series of trains for the national event. The Duke of Wellington, Prime Minister, and his entourage were allocated a special coach and the trains, headed by *Rocket*, departed amid a fanfare of trumpets. Their first stop was at Rainhill for the engines to be replenished with water. As they waited there, William Huskisson, who had political differences with the duke, decided to make amends. He got out of his coach onto the track to go forward

Two views of trains on the Liverpool & Manchester Railway. Above, open third-class carriages hauled by a locomotive of the *Rocket* class. Below, first-class carriages. They were designed to look like stagecoaches. Private coaches might be transported on flat wagons. Second class were like thirds but with a canopy roof.

and make contact with him. Unfortunately, just at that moment, another train passed by on that line and severed Huskisson's leg. He died in agony a few hours later. The procession continued after a delay but without the rejoicing that had been intended. It returned late amidst heavy rain to a dampening conclusion. However, the railway had proved its viability and set in motion the construction of a host of others. Within ten years, it would be possible to travel by train from Manchester and Liverpool via Birmingham to London.

Phenomenal Growth

Following the proven success, both practically and financially, of the Liverpool & Manchester Railway, other towns, particularly in Lancashire, vied to be connected to the line for passenger traffic. In addition, merchants and industrialists saw huge opportunities for expanding their businesses. A spate of proposals reached Parliament and the Lancashire network grew rapidly. Only a year after the opening of the Liverpool & Manchester Railway, a branch had been constructed from it to Warrington in the south, with a through connection to Bolton added the following year, and the year after that to Wigan. This was extended in 1838 to Preston, and in the same year it was possible to travel from Bolton to Manchester by rail. By then, the Grand Junction Railway had been completed from Birmingham to connect with the Liverpool & Manchester Railway at Warrington, making through journeys possible to London via the London & Birmingham Railway. The Manchester & Leeds line was opened in 1839 and by 1840 the route north from Preston had reached Lancaster. Taking into consideration the planning and construction work involved, this was phenomenal growth in a mere ten years.

In 1846 a line from Preston to Blackburn and Burnley was opened and the line from Lancaster reached the northern borders of the county on its way to Carlisle. Links in the west to and from Liverpool were slower in coming but by 1850 direct lines had been opened between there and Bolton, Preston and Southport. By then, South Lancashire enjoyed the most concentrated network in the country. You had the choice of eleven trains from Liverpool to Manchester each day, first, second or third class, and an express could speed you there in fifty minutes on your way to Leeds. You could also catch eleven trains a day from Blackburn to Liverpool, with a choice of two different routes and a quickest journey time of one hour and twenty-five minutes. In 2022, the equivalent journey by train took one minute longer! However, it was not until 1857 that a line was opened from the main line at Carnforth through to Barrow, the furthest outlier of the Historic County of Lancashire. Within a few years, most of the individual railways that had constructed the lines were amalgamated into the Lancashire & Yorkshire Railway, the London & North Western Railway or the Furness Railway, which were themselves incorporated in the London, Midland & Scottish Railway in 1923.

A Political Machine

William Howitt, visiting the the east Lancashire uplands in 1838, remarked on the woeful appearance of the countryside and cottages compared to the rest of the country. At bad times like these, the Chartist movement, which campaigned for political rights for the working class, was at its strongest. That same year, a crowd of 50,000 massed on Kersal Moor near Manchester. Although a stock of arms was collected to force a revolution, their aims for reforming the political system failed to catch on. The workers were not interested in emancipation but alleviation of their pressing physical needs. The leaders were arrested or fled. Some turned to the Anti-Corn Law League, which aimed at overthrowing the Corn Laws that maintained the price for farmers but caused hardship for others. This was described by *The Times* as 'the most political machine this country has yet seen'. It was supported (although not unanimously) by the Manchester Chamber of Commerce, which had emerged as Lancashire's first commercial organisation in 1820. Success followed in the repeal of the Corn Laws in 1846, which was championed by local heroes Richard Cobden, a Mancunian calico manufacturer, and John Bright, a Quaker and Rochdale carpet manufacturer. The victory was commemorated by the Free Trade Hall in Manchester.

NO ADULTERATION

Several Chartists joined with others on a momentous occasion in the evening of 1 December 1844 to open the first store of the Rochdale Friendly Co-operative Society. It was the most successful of all nineteenth-century working-class movements. The entire stock of butter, sugar, flour, oatmeal and candles was sold out and the dividends shared out among members. You could be assured of a fair price for a good article. A huge advantage was that the food was not dangerous or poisonous; no toxic bulking agents added by unscrupulous tradesmen. Colouring food to disguise adulteration was also eliminated, but the public – so used to the artifical colours in disguised goods – had to be re-educated to recognise and accept the real thing. Rochdale's success inspired others, who engaged enthusiastically in the committee work to manage the administration. Only seven years later, there were 130 societies and 15,000 members. Twelve years after that, the North of England Co-operative Wholesale Society was formed in Manchester.

You can imagine the scene. You arrive at a grocer's at seven o'clock on a Saturday evening and queue to get into a crowded shop. Men are giving up their visit to the pub and accompanying their wives and children (greatly reducing the incidence of alcoholism). Shoemakers, cloggers and tailors are at work. A clerk is at hand to manage the accounts. A watch club collects weekly payments, drawn by lot that night to decide who shall have a repeater that sounds the time. Upstairs, a newsroom is available with newspapers and periodicals. A librarian is busy lending out 200 books that night to members and their sons, wives and daughters. Such might be Xanthippe, named after the wife of the Greek philosopher Socrates. She and her sister Pandora (a Greek goddess), listed as factory children, were the daughters of a weaver who had a passion for ancient history[14].

Frederic Harrison, a London Lawyer, came to Lancashire in 1863 on a fact-finding mission about the cotton famine. He was most impressed by a committee meeting of a Co-op store, which discussed business 'in a very quiet, sensible and intelligent way' with 'great business skill'[15]. However, the manager of a Co-operative store in Manchester was a radical in politics and a keen Chartist. He had put all his money into a Co-operative mill but expected to lose it. He had no faith in trade unions and as a Manchester man could not work in Oldham or elsewhere for jealousy. He thought the cotton trade was ruined and expected to lose all his money in it, but he was against emigration as it drew off the best men and the country then lost them.

A Worn Sovereign

No wonder workers flocked to the co-operatives if they were the victims of a 'trucking' scam at the mill, where masters obliged them to buy provisions and clothes at inflated prices. In some instances, in remote areas without shops, the facility could be a boon, but charges might be extortionate. Worse, the workers' wages might be paid in kind, not money, and the process managed by a member of the master's family. In this scenario (contrast with the Co-op), you are given a sovereign in pay at the counting house. You then go upstairs to the shop and the coin is handed in for credit there to the profit of the owner. The sovereign is popped into a tube and goes downstairs to be reused by the next worker/customer. The only joke is that the head and tail of the sovereign will be worn off and rendered unusable and worthless for the master in the end. Seriously, at one time, in 1842, the truck system operated in all the mills between Manchester and Haslingden, except one. There, under the free system, the workers were noticeably better dressed and their houses better furnished. They shopped around and became more independent.

However, the vast majority, who were in thrall to their masters, accepted without question what they received in lieu of their wages and resorted to gambling in the hope of building up savings. When their husbands were away to attend meetings, wives would steal away from their houses to organise a raffle, with the winner taking home some independent means. When the market was brisk, the masters might bundle cheeses into people's houses and deduct the supposed value from their pay. Workers (boys and men) might be given a wage ticket, which they had to take to a public house owned by the firm. The landlord changed it for cash with a cut to be spent on beer, and the firm got their wage money back. The pub stayed open until past midnight and the boys would go home drunk. If someone insisted on coin instead of drink, a complaint would be made about his work. The practice was outlawed in Britain by a series of Truck Acts starting in 1725 and culminating in 1940.

Good and Bad Masters

It is said that as early as the late eighteenth century spinning mills in Preston used apprentice or orphan labour from the Foundling Hospital in London. The reformer Joseph Livesey described them as 'poor, squalid deformed beings with crooked legs from standing 12 hours at a time'[16] like 'West Indian slavery'. Who were the masters who could enforce such slavery? At first, they were just weavers, spinners or farmers who saved up enough money to progress into business. Many kept up their existing way of life with strict and regular hours, simple food and clothing, wearing clogs to the end. However, others wanted to distance themselves from their own class. They would send their children to boarding school to polish up their accent and absorb upper-class manners and social connections. However, they were not necessarily happy, divorced from their own kind but not accepted by those they sought to join. Some saw their success as a sign of approval, others were unable to progress in practice, or aspiration, from penny pinching to political awareness. Thomas Darwell built up the large Sovereign Mills in Wigan at the start of the eighteenth century. He was reprimanded by the Home Office when the *Wigan Advertiser* reported that children under 16 were working from

5 a.m. until 9 p.m. Some (!) were allowed to go home for breakfast and dinner. When an anonymous letter (from 'your sworn enemy') appeared in the press, threatening that 'the distress of the poor cries aloud for your blood', Thomas put up posters offering a 50 guinea reward (two years' wages) for 'information that will lead to the conviction of the writer' The poster can be seen in reproduction in Aspin's *The First Industrial Society: Lancashire, 1750-1850*. He was twice Mayor of Wigan and lived in Ince Hall before leasing the even grander Standish Hall, but his business failed and he died in poverty.

There were, however, model mills and mill owners. In the early days there was a contest between two manufacturers as to who would pay the higher wages. The winner received a silver cup subscribed by his employees. Some anticipated and fought for the 1842 Act on working conditions. Others provided schools for children of employees. One established contributions towards a scheme for sick leave with pay. At one factory, the workers were able to stop work and look out of the windows at the countryside and the spectacle of huntsmen following a hare. They were allowed to bring guns to work and go out to shoot birds that they spotted. They could enjoy the fruits of the mill yard, which was like an orchard, and cultivate their own fruit and vegetables. They could place seeds on top of the steam pipes to force growth and compete in growing the earliest and biggest cucumber. Other owners provided well-maintained cottages at reasonable rents or a washroom with soap, towels and combs. Annual treats might be provided with a band, dancing, lantern show, fireworks and sumptuous feast. Fortunate were these few!

GOLDEN ANNIVERSARY CELEBRATIONS AND A BOXING MATCH

In 1849 a lavish entertainment was laid on for the workers and friends of Low Moor Mill, near Clitheroe. Jeremiah Garnett was the senior partner of the firm and he was celebrating the fifty years his family had been in the business. For a dinner enjoyed by 500 guests, an ox had been slaughtered, which was accompanied by many other meats and rich plum puddings. After a tea on the same scale, about a thousand people attended a grand ball at which 'factory operatives, gentlemen and ladies' mingled in 'perfect amity'.[17] Industrial relations had not been so smooth and became increasingly strained by the introduction of steam power. In 1826 the firm had threatened to fire on rioters with a cannon. Three years later, during the severe trade depression of 1829, it was reported that the firm was intending to build a moat round the premises to render them impregnable.

In 1858, nine years after the great party, James Garnett, Jeremiah's great-nephew, became a partner in the Low Mill concern and began to write a diary. John Ward, a weaver at the same mill at the same time, kept a diary from 1 April 1860 to 4 December 1864. The diaries, therefore, are of particular and remarkable interest as views, written from an owner's perspective, are paralleled by those of a worker at the same establishment.

You can imagine them sparring with each other in the form of a boxing match, match. Diary entries have been paraphrased to form a narrative with some quotes verbatim in extracted sections '*thus*'.

James Garnett v John Ward Round 1
In the blue corner: James Garnett

One of my workers has left work without giving notice. The magistrates have ordered him to pay the costs and return to work or go to the Preston House of Correction for a month. Abraham Pinder, the first Organising Secretary of the Amalgamated Power-Loom Weavers, enters the scene, representing his workers.

I hope for prosperity in 1859 as employment is easily provided at good wages. It turns out to be a year of wage disputes and strikes. A strike at Padiham leads to a 5 per cent increase in wages there. This piles pressure on the manager here at Low Moor and gives encouragement to the workers for them to receive the same. There are difficulties dealing with the quality of the cotton and the spinners and weavers are going on strike. They are soon returning to work. A lad has been stopped for making bad work and the weavers have gone on strike again. Dust and wages are also an issue. The strike has been settled after three days by negotiation with Abraham Pinder.

The problem has been exacerbated by different demands from a proliferation of operatives. Although weavers and spinners predominate, hands in the blow room have given notice and there have been deputations from winders, warpers, twisters and card room workers. Once again Pinder, has negotiated a complicated dispute, this time between the management and weavers, which settled for '½d per cent' advance on the standard rate of pay for all kinds of cloth. A better rate of pay agreed in one area or one local employer or group of operatives is being used by other employees to further their demands. When rovers [who load cotton onto bobbins] and slubbers [who stain the cotton)]secured an increase in pay, the weavers followed. I sent for Abraham, who negotiated another 5 per cent increase with a reduction of ¼d on the advance on the standard rate, but he has now been dismissed by the executive Committee of the Weavers' Union in connection with charges of embezzlement. This was just when his negotiating skills were needed even more.

In the red corner: John Ward

I went to the annual meeting of the Weavers' Uunion and was chosen President, '*a very high honour*'. Living at the time in Clitheroe, I went to see my brother in Manchester but discovered he had gone to live in Preston without letting me know. So I walked to where he had lived as a boy near Hyde and Newton Moor. It was twenty-eight years since I had gone that way but everything had changed.

> *Villages have grown into large towns, and country places where there was nothing but fields are now covered with streets, and*

> villages and large factories and workshops everywhere. I made
> enquires [at] many a place after people who had lived there, but
> they were either dead or gone to America or gone somewhere
> else. I only saw one woman I knew, but she did not know me
> and would not believe me when I told her I was very tired.
> When I got to Ashton and could find nobody that I knew, I
> took the omnibus to Manchester, and all the way back I could
> see that it was all one town from Audenshaw to Manchester.

I disagree with the demands of the workers, which have been carried by a large majority. I am keeping in touch with the progress of the Reform Bill through the House of Commons by going up to Clitheroe and reading the newspaper there or bringing one home. I am taking a great interest in the campaign of Garibaldi in Sicily, recording in some detail his campaign through Sicily and the Italian mainland over several months The Prince of Wales [future Edward VII] is just 'sporting through Canada'. Much of my time is spent in collecting, banking and distributing money for men on strike, especially in Colne and Bolton. There have been large fund raising meetings of over one thousand weavers and one 'camp' meeting of 4,000. I am continually chairing union meetings of deputies, composing committee reports and posting them.

Relations between the two sides have hardened. The Colne masters have brought families from Coventry [where families were in distress because of slack in the ribband trade] and threatened to use them as strike breakers. I have made many rail journeys and walks in between, often in atrocious weather with deep snow, bitter cold and heavy rain. Once the River Ribble rose so high that it overflowed the waterwheel and power for the mill was lost. On another occasion, deep snow caused my train to run late into Blackburn and miss the connection to Clitheroe. One of the passengers had to go into work in the morning or lose time altogether. I accompanied him on the 11-mile walk through knee-deep snow and when he got home his shoes were frozen to his feet. The rest of the company were forced to stay the night in Blackburn and tried to get the expense refunded through the unsympathetic stationmaster. A dispute arose, which, with my experience, I eagerly took up with the railway company.

At the end of the year 1860 I have assessed my condition compared with the preceding year [like Pepys 200 years before]: 'I have better clothes, better furniture and better bedding, and my daughter has more clothes than she ever had in her life; and as long as we have good health and plenty of work we will do well enough.' I have read of the election of 'Mr Lincoln President' [21 January 1861].

James Garnett v John Ward, Round 2
In the blue corner: James Garnett

Following two years of prosperity, industrial relations have become more fraught with the advent of the American Civil War. The supply of cotton has dried up and the price risen by 50 per cent. The markets in India and China are reluctant to buy and overproduction means that staff have had to be shed. A proposed reduction in wages of as much as 10 per cent has led to a dispute over the possibility of short-time working. Discussions have broken down and strikes called. Union funds have been used to alleviate hardship and unemployment. People have started to look for work elsewhere. The cotton market is volatile. News comes slowly by ship, taking ten to twelve days to cross the Atlantic, so immediate and effective action is inhibited. There are fears for conflict locally and internationally.

As the fortunes of the war fluctuate, so have the hopes of the employers and workers, sometimes for the Confederates of the cotton-producing South and at other times for the Federates [Union] of the North. At Low Moor Mill, arbitration has failed and one of the union committee has been victimised and dismissed. However, speculation by Liverpool merchants has harvested rich profits. Cotton from India has proved to be inferior, but the price of that has risen too, and supplies have been sought from China and Egypt.

Agreement has been reached on four days a week working and my family have been able to enjoy partridge shooting. The winter of 1862–63 has been bleak. The mill has been closed and a relief committee organised to help the unemployed in the form of cash, food, clothing, bedding and fuel. Schools have been established for boys and girls out of work. We have contributed to the relief efforts in money and kind. A ship has arrived at Liverpool with supplies of cotton from the Federate [Union] side. Now the war has ended (in 1865), prices have fallen, full production has been resumed but the workers have been emboldened to ask for a restoration of pay levels.

In the red corner: John Ward

Four days after the news of the election of Abraham Lincoln as President of the United States and the start of the American Civil War, a notice has been put up in the mill. It announced a reduction in wages as the price of cotton had risen in speculative fear that there would be no crop the following year. The Clitheroe weavers have decided to ask for the same terms as Blackburn – that is, four days a week at 5 per cent reduction, which could be afforded because of the economies of scale of the large mills there. Clitheroe masters answered that they could not afford it and so their weavers have gone on strike.

Two weeks later Blackburn have returned to work. I spoke to the largest meeting that I have ever addressed asking for help for Clitheroe, followed by speakers from Bolton, Darwen and Colne. I have been involved in meeting after meeting held to ascertain the help needed for the separate areas and apportion strike pay to alleviate the distress of individuals. I went to Preston to borrow and distribute strike pay. An abortive meeting with unofficial mediators broke up in confusion when they were pelted with stones, shoved, kicked and abused. Official mediation has failed and the weavers, faced with starvation, have returned to work after five weeks but over 100 looms are idle. Renewed arbitration has gone to an umpire's judgement, but the terms were rejected by the masters.

One of the committee was discharged for being a ringleader and they *'seem determined to get rid of every committee man ... as all the blame is attached to them for resisting the reduction of ten per cent'*. A victim fund has been set up to help them.

My term of office as President has expired but I have been elected on to the committee for six months. Although the men have returned to work, there were stoppages because of breakdowns and the Ribble running low because of dry weather. This has continued for two weeks, but flood water has failed to create the backwater needed to turn the wheel. For months I have been reading the papers avidly and anxiously for news of the American Civil War. I have taken a five pound share in the construction of a co-operative spinning and weaving factory. I have paid a penny per week into the Mechanics and Reading Room at Low Moor near the mill *'so I will see a daily paper regular'*. At the end of 1861: *'I am not so well off as I have been for several years.'* At the start of 1862:

> *We are working short time and owing to the scarcity of cotton we are working with such rubbish as I never was in my life. I had a very narrow escape with my life this morning. The shaft above my head broke and fell just as I was coming from under it. As it is it broke a great deal of yarn.*

[In June 1862 the diary breaks off, to be resumed in April 1864 as illustrated. He writes]:

> *I now take up my pen to resume the task. It has been a very poor time for me all the time owing to the American war, which seems as far off as being settled as ever. The mill I work in was stopped all last winter, during which time I had three shillings per week allowed by the relief committee, which barely kept me alive. When we started work again it was with Surat cotton [of poor quality from India], and a great number of weavers can only mind two looms. We can earn very little.*

John Ward's diary entry for 10 April 1864. See text for transcription. (Courtesy Lancashire Archives)

I have not earned a shilling a day this last month, and there are many like me. My clothes and bedding is wearing out very fast and I have no means of getting any more, as what wages I get does hardly keep me, after paying rent, rates and firing. I am living by myself ... If things do not mend this summer I will try somewhere else or something else ... They have promised us better work as soon as the cotton is done that they have on hand. They have promised so often that we can hardly believe them.

Complaints by the workers to the masters have met with the response that they could leave if they wished (September 1864). There is no sign of any cotton coming and winter is at hand. The mill is running half-time. Now (in October) it has stopped altogether for a week. The mill has now restarted full time for weavers, four days a week for others, with supplies for another three weeks.

There are poor prospects for Christmas.

Referee's Decision: Level on Points
James Garnett seems to have been a reasonable master. Certainly, John Ward has nothing personally critical to say about him when many masters were cruel and sadistic. John himself tried hard to settle disputes in an amicable way without violence.

ITS HEIGHT WAS REDUCED BY 100FT BUT IT STILL COLLAPSED

A building boom changed the face of the landscape. Manufacturers strove to prove superiority over their rivals by the height of their chimneys. In 1842, a 367½ft-high one was built by Blinkhorn's Chemical Works in Bolton, in the space of sixteen weeks. Before it came into use, 4,000 people were wound up in a basket inside, four at a time, to the top to view the surrounding countryside. Two years later, Mr Dobb started a chimney in his chemical works in Wallgate, Wigan, that rose to 435ft. However, cracks appeared at the base. It was reduced in height by a 100ft but collapsed. The chimney at India Mill, Darwen, completed in 1867, was smaller at only 300ft but outdid all its rivals in beauty. Designed to look like the Campanile in St Mark's Square in Venice, it can be admired to this day. Thirty-five horses were needed to pull the immense stone on which it was based along a special road to the site.

The size of the mills varied in time and place. In Blackburn in 1843, the average number of workers in a mill was 281, whereas Bolton had only 217, Bury 162 and Oldham 79. By 1895 the average number of looms was 603 and this rose to 822 in 1912. During the Edwardian period massive redbrick mills were built, thirty-two of them with more than 1,000 looms. Ninety per cent of Blackburn's cloth was exported to the Far East in 1900, then India started to manufacture its own.

Drink, Temperance and Education

For centuries weak beer was the staple, safe drink for farming communities throughout the land. In Lancashire, this harmless and healthful habit was dissipated by the Industrial Revolution to produce a distinct, polarised culture.

By the start of the eighteenth century, farm workers had been tempted from the fields, far and wide, to join in the prosperity generated by the revolution of the cotton industry. Many mill workers had formed a pattern of life that alternated from amassing newfound wealth to spending it on a bout of drinking. Women, boys and girls would join the men in a favourite pastime of drunkenness, as in Manchester to celebrate the Coronation of 1821 and New Year's Day 1831. On Easter Day, 1832, thousands of young people flooded into Bolton intent on intoxication and riotous exploits. This habit worked well in times of prosperity, but when hard times arrived, excessive drinking became an unaffordable solace with disastrous results. The most violent fluctuation hit in 1861 with the outbreak of the American Civil War. While the Northern states, assisted by the Royal Navy, strove to blockade any exports, the Southern Confederate states aimed paradoxically to overthrow the British economy by allowing cotton to rot on Southern wharfs. A Southern senator pronounced: 'England would topple and carry the whole world with her ... Cotton is King.' In Lancashire 384,000 cotton employees faced starvation. Many sympathised with the South and a secret envoy, Andrew Dunwoody Bulloch, arranged for the construction on Merseyside of armed ships, most notably the *Alabama*, to prey on 'allied' shipping. The British government under Palmerston remained neutral but within a year, 247,000 operatives were out of work and a further 485,434 were reliant on relief. New supplies were sourced from India and Egypt. It took three years for American cotton imports to be restored and for Lancashire to enjoy the benefits.

In the meantime, a strong temperance movement had emerged. It was the first great propaganda movement of modern times and was one of the most remarkable achievements of social change in the nineteenth century. The virtues of abstinence had been preached in Salford as early as 1809; a pamphlet issued there ten years later led to the first teetotal pledge in 1832. But it was Joseph Livesey of Preston, a successful businessman in the cheese market, who was its most skilled propagandist and gave the movement the greatest impetus. Not only did he organise a procession with band and banners to support the movement but he publicised the event, picturing himself riding in a carriage with cheering crowds. He was opposed by his implacable political opponent Thomas Batty Addison, a Tory of extreme views who argued that many paupers were the slaves of the habits of drink and tobacco. A lecture in 1832 led to the signing by the 'Seven Men of Preston', who pledged total abstinence. The term teetotal was adopted there the following year in a meeting at the cockpit.

Alternative entertainment was devised, particularly tea parties, to draw people away from pubs and shops. Magazines contained recipes for non-alcoholic drinks. A temperance festival lasting a week was organised. Missionaries set out from Preston to convert towns as far and wide as Blackburn, Rochdale and Stockport. Manchester carpenter John Cassel became a missionary for the cause, which he furthered by printing tracts and publishing journals, the forerunner to his great publishing firm. Two years later, the movement could boast 2,000 teetotallers and the year after that a national temperance conference was held in Preston with a procession of 10,000. Hymns and songs were composed: 'Water pure doth brighter shine/Than brandy, rum or sparkling wine.' While the movement failed to achieve its aims of total abolition, it did play a part in the eventual widespread adoption of moderate drinking.

Lectures were part of the abolitionist programme of reform, which attracted up to 3,000 devotees at open-air meetings. In 1842 the mills were closed and the workers were starving as a result of the Plug Plot Riots, when workers and Chartists who had intended removing drain plugs from new boilers in order to sabotage them were confronted by soldiers. A group of young men, funded by a small subscription, hired a room and formed the Royton Temperance Seminary. They built up a library and gave religious and secular instruction to several hundred children at a nearby mill. Twenty years later, the founders had benefited from their own learning to become teachers, master cotton spinners, foremen and mill managers in Russia. Similar societies sprang up in every Lancashire town and most villages. Lectures at Mechanics Institutes attracted large crowds, as at the first public lecture in Manchester when a crowd of 1,400 filled the room to capacity and the lecture had to be repeated later. In a pioneering outreach of the Warrington Institute in 1858, a van pulled by one horse and filled with books travelled around the town once a week. It was almost certainly the first mobile ('perambulating') library. When the Manchester Free Library opened in 1852, a policeman had to control the crowd round the desk from which books were issued ranging from philosophy to mechanics, history and astronomy.

Sunday school classes and church attendance instilled standards of behaviour. Discipline might be enforced by shaming methods unthinkable today, for example hanging cards with 'dunce', 'careless' or 'swearer' around pupils' necks and standing them in a 'stall of repentance' in front of the superintendent's desk. Statistics showed that church and chapel provision and attendance at Sunday school was significantly higher in Lancashire than London. Mill owners built churches, which their employees were encouraged to attend and where they were regaled with sermons on the virtues of hard work and thrift. Both sides would be encouraged by the hope of rewards in the afterlife.

GLADSTONE AND SLAVERY

The cotton industry was founded on slavery, although the Lancashire weavers were hardly aware or cared about it. Much of their condition was equally brutal and inescapable. The section of the population that gained most directly from it, besides the manufacturing community, were Liverpool merchants. Their income was derived from the triangular trade: manufactured goods to Africa, slaves from there to America and cotton back home. The profit of the town, and therefore its prosperity, increased enormously during the eighteenth century and laid the foundations for its immense wealth during Victorian times.

There were abolitionists, most notably the polymath and banker William Roscoe. There were also some not directly involved in the slave trade, like the family of John Foster and his sons. John Foster Junior took over from his father, John Senior, as chief surveyor of the docks in 1824. However, both of them benefited from the expansion of the docks during their reign over these money-making projects. Galling for those who suffered from the practice and those who opposed it, was the compensation from the government for the loss of income when abolition came. Equally galling must have been the praise given on expensive memorials for the good works and benefactions coming from those who had amassed money through slave trading. For many years, families whose fortune and fame accrued from the slave trade have not recognised or openly admitted the advantage they thereby gained.

Such was the family of John Gladstone, father of William Ewart Gladstone. John, a Scot, moved to Liverpool, like many of his compatriots, to take advantage of the trading opportunities there. Starting with grain, he dealt in tobacco from Virginia, USA, and other goods from the West Indies. Although he was involved in only one slave voyage when 395 Africans were kidnapped and transported to the Bahamas, he owned plantations in Jamaica and British Guiana. Under the terms of the Slavery Abolition Act of 1835, he received compensation of

William Ewart Gladstone in full flow at the Dispatch Box in the House of Commons. (Private collection)

over £112,716 for the 2,912 slaves he had been obliged to free. He became an MP, as did three of his sons, and was created a baronet. During his lifetime he paid for the construction of three churches and contributed to the cost of two schools and left in his will enough to pay for many more. He is honoured by a monument commissioned by his widow and children 'with the deepest feeling of reverence and regret'. It stands in the Oratory just by the entrance to Liverpool's Anglican Cathedral and shows him sitting cross-legged and comfortable in an armchair, eagerly expounding something from a paper he holds. The inscription adds: 'an intelligent, indefatigable and successful merchant, a virtuous and amiable man'. One of his children, second son Robertson, was also a West Indies merchant and sugar importer (and became Mayor of Liverpool). His fourth son William Ewart Gladstone, four times Prime Minister, was born in fashionable Rodney Street in the centre of Liverpool, grew up in a luxurious family home on an estate outside the town and went to Eton. In 2020, the University of Liverpool announced that they would remove his name from one of their student accommodation blocks. In 2023, family descendants travelled to Africa to apologise and make reparations.

Heaven on Earth

Kitty Wilkinson is best remembered for her work in Liverpool to combat the cholera epidemic of 1832. Against all personal difficulties, she supplied washing and sanitising facilities to the poor, which led to the first public baths in the world. Her work as a helper of the poor is praised in a memorial window in the Lady Chapel of Liverpool's Anglican Cathedral.

She was born of an Irish family who sailed to Liverpool in 1794 to make a new and better life, as millions were to do in the nineteenth century. Like many others, tragedy struck on the way. Within sight of the coast, their boat was shipwrecked.

Kitty's mother and her younger brother were saved but her father and infant sister were drowned. When Kitty was about 11 years old, her mother became so ill that she had to go into the infirmary. To save the family from the dreaded workhouse, Kitty was indentured for ten years to a mill at Caton near Lancaster. Unusually, the owner seems to have been exceptionally kind, providing an airing ground and library. Later she was able to speak of her experience in glowing terms, 'If ever there was a heaven on earth, it was that apprentice house, where we were brought up in such ignorance of evil, and where the manager of the mill was father to us all.' In fact, although most of the sixty-eight children under 18 years of age attended school and all those over 10 could read, the mill used to work its labour force for twelve and a half hours a day with only a quarter of an hour for breakfast and three-quarters of an hour for dinner. Maybe Kitty's favourable memories were coloured by the physical and mental hardships of her later life in Liverpool.

When she returned to Liverpool, Kitty opened a school to support her frail mother but was then forced to supplement her income by shovelling horse manure from the streets to be sold to farmers. She married a French Catholic seaman. Two children were born before he too was drowned at sea. For ten years Kitty worked as a single parent, manufacturing nails and shovelling manure but always helping the poor. Then she remarried, to Thomas Wilkinson, eight years her junior. A few weeks later, they adopted four orphaned children. At least thirty-seven adoptions have been recorded in her name. At this point, Kitty's mother and brother died. He had been ill from birth. Soon after, the cholera epidemic struck, killing 53 per cent of the children under 5 years of age in 1846. It coincided with the potato famine in Ireland. The population of Liverpool was swelled by the consequent mass migration. Kitty was at work helping her neighbours to disinfect and wash the clothes and bedding of the diseased. Starting with a large copper container in her kitchen, she opened a washhouse with clean water and disinfectant for eighty-five families a week at a small charge. She formed an infant school for twenty children and looked after other orphaned children, once five at a time, while their father went to sea to earn money. After ten years, the Corporation followed Kitty's example and opened their public baths and washhouse. When she was 60, Queen Victoria presented her with a silver teapot service and she and Thomas were appointed superintendents of the new baths. Thomas died two years later, but Kitty worked on for another eight years until she was retired, without a pension. She died aged 74 in 1860. William Rathbone, MP and Freeman of Liverpool, her friend and supporter, was present at her interment. Her simple gravestone reads:

> Indefatigable and Selfdenying
> She was the Widows Friend
> The support of the Orphan.
> The Fearless and Unwearied
> Nurse of the Sick: the Originator
> For Baths and Wash houses for
> The Poor

She is also commemorated by a window in the Lady Chapel of Liverpool's Anglican Cathedral and by the first and only statue of a woman in the gallery of great Liverpudlians in St George's Hall.

Relief

In 1863 many thousands of men were without their regular means of livelihood and most of them had been idle or drawing relief for well over a year. Frederic Harrison, who had come from London to report on the situation, observed the distribution of relief to 300 people and five meetings of unemployed working men. His opinion in general was that the central and critical problem of the North was not lack of food but 'the silent wasting away of civilized and manly life ... the loss of pride and decency ... the *moral* starvation ...'[18] The supply of raw cotton would not improve in the near future due to the ongoing American Civil War and the relief fund would be exhausted in six to eight months. Two shillings a week per person would supply soup, bread and a little tea, sugar or cheese but no meat, with no allowance for rent. Family income had been well over twenty times as much (£4 a week), which shows how their standard of living had plummeted. In some districts poor-quality Surat cotton from India was introduced but the men could only earn a fraction of their previous earnings and refused to work. They then lost their relief money and were driven back to work by hunger. However, girls (who did not know 'the head from the point of a needle') were forced into education. They practised making dresses out of odds and ends and took it in turns to cook in a soup kitchen providing dinner for a penny. The boys learnt writing and arithmetic.

Word spread to Australia via passenger and trade vessels of the calamitous state of Lancashire workers and relief money was raised there through public meetings, religious institutions and workers' organisations. New South Wales colony alone contributed £20,000 to the fund. The money was distributed through the chosen agents in a scheme co-ordinated by Sir J.P. Kay-Shuttleworth. The Australian money was devoted to establishing day schools, providing classes in practical subjects, paying school pence for destitute children and giving material aid through well-organised local committees. However, this was not well received in Australia, where there was strong support for helping families to emigrate and start a new life there instead.

Kay-Shuttleworth had been born James Kay in Rochdale and settled in Manchester, where he gained experience of the conditions of the poor in Lancashire factory districts. Embarking on a political career, he administered the Government Grant for Public Education in Britain. He retired from this due to ill health but was called by Lord Derby to manage the relief fund. He had changed his name by royal licence to Kay-Shuttleworth after his marriage to Janet Shuttleworth, heiress of Gawthorpe Hall near Burnley. This had been built for the Shuttleworth family in 1600–05 with Elizabethan panelling and plasterwork of outstanding quality. The couple restored the hall in the 1850s, employing Sir Charles Barry in collaboration with A.W. Pugin. These two outstanding architects were also working on the restoration of the Palace of Westminster in London at a time when Sir James was in office there. Gawthorpe is the only country house in which Barry and Pugin collaborated, producing a collection rich in Gothic Revival furniture, metalwork and textiles.

Cotton Exchanges

The scale and complexity of the cotton industry increased exponentially through the nineteenth century. This produced radical solutions to streamline the system. Liverpool pioneered cotton forward trading at the beginning of the nineteenth century. This spread to the manufacturers themselves, who eventually used this process rather than on-the-spot dealing and settling. Centres were needed where business could be conducted collectively and efficiently. Blackburn paved the way by laying a foundation stone for a cotton exchange in the early 1860s but only half was built because of the American Civil War and the trade depression. In 1873, the Liverpool Cotton Brokers' Association established the first commodity market in Europe to develop futures trading, anticipating present-day hedge funds. Sir William Forwood, who was successful in many other areas in Liverpool's commerce and politics, dismissed it as a 'most dangerous trade'. It was indeed liable to huge fluctuations in demand and profit. In 1883 there was a spectacular bankruptcy of an American, Morris Ranger, after twice cornering the Liverpool market.

When Liverpool built its third exchange for the commodity in 1906, its size and outstanding magnificence truly represented cotton's importance for the prosperity of the city at the time. The Royal Exchange in Manchester dealt only in foreign cotton trade but a final extension to the building in 1913 housed 10,000 subscribers. It was the nerve centre and powerhouse of the industry. Lancashire was at the height of its cotton fortunes: 81 per cent of the cotton produced was exported, 21 per cent to India, a proportion that was to be dramatically reversed in the next half-century. Liverpool's exchange was downsized in the 1960s and much of its main façade destroyed in an act of architectural vandalism, symbolic of the reality of the moment. Fortunately, a new use was found for the Royal Exchange in Manchester and its magnificent interior was preserved as a thriving theatre. The final day's trading prices are still on view as a reminder of its past glory.

8

VICTORIAN PHILANTHROPY, PLEASURE AND PAIN

BUILD AT ANY COST

Historic England's grades have been used to select Victorian town halls and indicate their architectural merit. ** indicates Grade I; * indicates Grade II*. These represent 2.5 per cent and 5.8 percent respectively of all listed buildings.

Lancashire towns vied with each other as a matter of public pride to build town halls that proclaimed their status and growing prosperity, from Barrow in the far north-west of the Historic County to Manchester, 100 miles in the south-east. The oldest town hall (built 1749–54) is Liverpool's**, a Georgian gem so elegant that it has never been replaced and it would seem sacrilege to do so. In its early days, it doubled up as the Exchange where merchants would conduct their business negotiations, and this has been replaced twice. Liverpool enhanced its image yet more by constructing St George's Hall**(illustrated on p146), described by the architectural historian Nikolaus Pevsner as one of the finest neo-Grecian buildings in the world.

There was a tradition of designing public buildings in a classical style, as opposed to the Gothic, and the neoclassical fashion continued in Liverpool long after the height of the Georgian period. St George's Hall was designed in 1840 by the young architect Harvey Lonsdale Elmes, who won two separate competitions for the Law Courts and an assembly hall. He

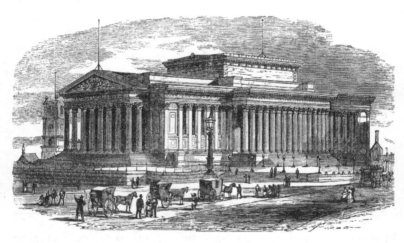

St George's Hall in neoclassical style. (Private collection)

Manchester Town Hall in neo-Gothic style. (Private collection)

combined them into a majestic unity, but he died young and his design had to be fully realised by the more famous Sir Charles Cockerell. Elmes designed only one other building of significance, Liverpool Collegiate School*, in a different, Gothic style.

Preston was not to be outdone. The foundation stone of Preston's third town hall (**?) was laid in 1862 and the most prestigious architect of the day, George Gilbert Scott, was engaged. He designed it in the almost obligatory Gothic style for such an edifice at the time. By then, Pugin's Gothic style had become de rigueur for ecclesiastical buildings and had then been used for the new Houses of Parliament, started in 1840. Preston's town hall burnt down in 1947 and was replaced in a more modern style. Had it survived, it certainly would have been listed Grade I.

Rochdale** initiated plans for a town hall as soon as the Rochdale Corporation was formed in 1858. It was a paragon of motivation and the unrealistic ambition of civic pride. The cost of an increasingly lavish Gothic style quadrupled by the time it was completed in 1871 and it was rated one of the finest municipal buildings in the country.

No wonder Manchester's town hall** is so grand (illustrated on p146). The Corporation demanded it be 'equal if not superior, to any similar building in the country at any cost which may be reasonably required'![19] It was designed by Alfred Waterhouse, who was the best architect of prestigious public buildings at the time. Planning for the new town hall had begun in 1863 and it was not completed until 1877. The main hall was described by John Ruskin, who at the time was considered to be the best critic of artistic excellence, as 'the most truly magnificent Gothic apartment in Europe'.

The Manchester area competition for those wishing to aggrandise themselves with a superior town hall was entered by Bolton* in 1866. It completed its strictly classical design with a high tower over a pedimented entrance in 1873. Accrington adopted the Peel Institute* as the area's town hall in 1868 when it gained borough status. Sporting a classical pedimented façade, it had opened ten years before as a memorial to Sir Robert Peel, Prime Minister.

In the mid-nineteenth century, Barrow* was little more than a small fishing village. However, after the discovery of iron ore in local mountains, a proposal was made as early as 1838 to link the area by a railway embankment across Morecambe Bay. With the establishment of a port in the town and a railway connection round the bay, Barrow became a municipal borough in 1867. Did it inspire Bootle* at the other end of the county to petition Parliament for the same status the following year? In 1877, architects were invited to submit proposals for a large civic building in Gothic style that would represent the growth and current stature of the town. It certainly did.

Lancaster's town hall* was designed in a classical style and opened in 1909. By the end of the nineteenth century the old town hall* (built 1781–83, now the museum) could not cope with the increasing administrative burden. The Corporation was unable to finance the new building but Lord Ashton, who with his father James Wiliamson had made a fortune out of lino, paid for it personally. He also bore the cost of the accompanying Queen Victoria Memorial* and a memorial** to his family overlooking the town and countryside.

Three Peels

As a young man, the first Robert Peel (later, the first Sir Robert) came home from selling milk in Blackburn to superintend cotton spinners working in his father's barn. The family took advantage of the pioneering spinning jenny, invented by Hargreaves in 1764–65. However, a mob, fearing for their livelihoods, destroyed their cottage in 1768 and then went on to ransack the new machinery. It is possible they were supported by the 'putters-out', whose livelihood would also have been damaged by the new machine. The factory was attacked again in 1779 and the jennies thrown into the river. Fleeing the town in disgust, Robert established a home and business in Bury. It was then and there that he again showed his interest in new applications for the development of the cotton industry by approaching Crompton to collaborate with him. Crompton, however, rebuffed him, having suffered from bad business deals in the past.

Sir Robert Peel's son, also Sir Robert Peel, was born there in 1788. Both Roberts affected the course of Lancashire history in many ways by their national political actions. The elder sponsored the 1819 Factory Act that prohibited under-9-year-olds from being employed. The younger attended the opening of the Liverpool & Manchester Railway, accompanying the then Prime Minister, the Duke of Wellington. Later, as Prime Minister himself from 1841 to 1846, Peel was responsible for the prohibition of women and boys from being employed underground in the mines and for reducing the hours of work to twelve hours for women and six and a half hours for children. It was his creation of a national police force that prompted the name of 'Bobby' for a policeman. Arguably, his greatest achievement was the repeal of the Corn Laws, which alleviated the threat of repeated starvation in Lancashire but coincided with his resignation in 1846.

Peel also campaigned vigorously for a park to be created in Salford. He secured government funding for the project and contributed generously himself. Opened in the same year, the park was named after him and a statue of him was erected there in a prominent position. He died in a riding accident in Hyde Park, London, in 1850 and is commemorated in a stone tower on Holcombe Hill above Ramsbottom, where his father's factory once stood. A plaque also marks the site of the family's original home in Cardwell Place in Blackburn. Coincidentally, the family's connection with Blackburn was renewed in 1884 when Sir Robert Peel, 3rd Baronet and son of the Prime Minister, was elected Conservative for the seat until 1886. It was unusual for an outsider to be elected for the town, but he did have historic connections.

From Chelsea to Manchester

Elizabeth Gaskell was born in Chelsea in 1810 and brought up in the genteel market town of Knutsford. She met a Unitarian minister in Manchester and married him in 1832. There she became acquainted with the poor of Manchester and their plight in times of hardship. Later on she was to write to a generous donor who contributed to a charity of hers to relieve the distress caused by the American cotton famine:

> We think of using part of it in allowing 6d or 8d a week to the poor old women, whom my daughters know *well*, – & who at present have only the workhouse allowance; barely enough for the cheapest, poorest food, – only just enough to keep life in. They have worked hard all their working years, poor old friendless women, and now crave and sicken after a 'taste of bacon' or something different to the perpetual oat-meal.

For most Mancunians, life was abominably harsh. Like so many of the towns that had sprung up during the cotton revolution, its growth was completely unplanned and unregulated. A local surgeon (Aspin, p.93) remarked that those who lived in the more populous areas 'could seldom hope to see the green face of nature'. Houses were built back to back without ventilation or drainage, so dark inside that candles were needed to light the way. In 1892 the sight of Manchester with the tall factory chimneys of the weaving mills rising above the masses of thick cloud stirred the Socialist Henry Hyndman[20] to remark on 'one hideous Malebolge [a circle of Dante's Inferno] of carbon laden fog and smoke ... this infernal pit of degradation'. Many families lived in two-room cellars with only one small window to let in the light. The kitchen led through to a bedroom in which a family of seven or eight would live and sleep, as many as five in a bed. In one street there was only one privy for 380 inhabitants. Rubbish was thrown onto dung heaps on which diseased pigs were fed. Waste filled the River Irwell so deep that it overflowed in heavy rain. Cholera was rife. In 1842, more than 57 per cent of children died before the age of 5.

Elizabeth Gaskell's first novel *Mary Barton*, published anonymously in 1848, portrayed these very times: of unrest and hardship for the workers and comparative ease and luxury for their employers. John Barton (fictional father of Mary) is imagined going to a trade union meeting. 'He had hesitated between the purchase of meal or opium, and had chosen the latter, for its use had become a necessity with him.'

Taking opium was the habit of another Manchester man of the period, this one non-fictional. Thomas De Quincy, born in Manchester in 1785, was a pupil at Manchester Grammar School, of which he writes, 'that school was variously distinguished. It was (1) ancient, having in fact been founded by a bishop of Exeter in an early part of the sixteenth century, so as now, in 1856, more than 300 years old; (2) it was rich, and was annually growing richer; and (3) it was dignified by a beneficial relation the University of Oxford.' Thomas was thus far removed from working-class Manchester contemporaries. However, having become an opium addict in London, he revisited Manchester and relates in *Confessions of an Opium Eater*:

> Some years ago, on passing through Manchester, I was informed by several cotton manufacturers that their workpeople were rapidly getting into the practice of opium-eating; so much so, that on a Saturday afternoon the counters of the druggists were strewed with pills of one, two or three grains, in preparation for the known demand of the evening. The immediate occasion of this practice was the lowness of wages, which, at that time, would not allow them to indulge in ale or spirits; and, wages rising, it would only be thought that this practice would cease: but ... those who always ate now ate the more.

In a later novel, *North and South*, Elizabeth Gaskell describes the difficulties from the employers' point of view, and *Wives and*

Daughters is set in a provincial town, based on her childhood in Knutsford. She met Dickens, Carlyle, Wordsworth and, above all, Charlotte Bronte, with whom she exchanged visits. Elizabeth was asked by Patrick Bronte to write Charlotte's biography when she died.

A COMMUNIST AND A MINISTER'S WIFE

Elizabeth Gaskell started writing *Mary Barton* in 1845 after the death of her infant son. In the same year that she describes the terrible living conditions of the time, two men could, for a few months, be seen sharing a table in Chetham's Library in Manchester overlooking a quiet courtyard. It was a meeting of minds that changed world history. Karl Marx had been studying in the British Museum and was invited by his friend Friedrich Engels to join him in Manchester. Together they studied revolutionary books, unobtainable in London, on political economy and the fate of English capitalism. These fed Marx's work, which influenced the success of Communism. He will have learnt from Engels the plight of the casual labourers of Ancoats. Engels certainly knew the squalor of living conditions, the pitiful child labour and the effects of industrial accidents on people lying in the infirmary or struggling along the streets of Manchester, describing it in his *Condition of the Working Class in England* as 'hell on earth'. ('Separate territories assigned to poverty. Removed from the sight of happier classes, poverty may struggle along as it can.') Marx will have been struck by the contrast and unfairness: his friend went off to enjoy the hunt in Cheshire while he benefited from the Mancunian wealth that supported them both. However, Engels experienced the economic panic of 1857 that seemed to presage the collapse of capitalism and the victory of the Communist millennium. A collapse did come a century later, but it was just Lancashire cotton.

Victorian Philanthropy, Pleasure And Pain

Chetham's Library, where Marx and Engels studied.

Spitting to Get into Prison

Lancashire can be proud of the part it played in the fight for political rights. Mancunians fought for fair representation in Parliament, particularly after the Peterloo Massacre of 1819. It was only after the Reform Act of 1832 that they were entitled to elect any MPs: two – the same as, for example, Clitheroe. Liverpool was not so vociferous, as it was controlled by a self-perpetuating Tory clique that was ended by the Reform Act of 1832 to favour Manchester. Although most Liverpool merchants benefited from the slave trade and fought hard for compensation when it finished, they were bravely opposed by many prominent citizens such as the Rathbone family and William Roscoe. The Liverpool abolitionist James Cropper built a school in Warrington to coincide with the declaration of emancipation in 1834.

In Manchester, an early memory of Emmeline Pankhurst was attending anti-slavery bazaars with her parents and her mother reading the abolitionist novel *Uncle Tom's Cabin*. She had been born in 1858 into a wealthy manufacturing and Liberal family who attended early Independent Labour Party meetings. In 1903, with her daughters Silvia and Christabel, she formed the Women's Social and Political Union (WSPU). The militant campaign of the Suffragettes began at a meeting in the Free Trade Hall in 1905. Winston Churchill and Sir Edward Grey, likely to be in the Cabinet if the Liberals won the forthcoming general election, were addressing the meeting when Christabel and a devoted follower interrupted the meeting and refused to be silenced. Christabel spat at one of the policemen who was trying to eject her, thus ensuring her arrest and imprisonment. The WSPU moved to London with Christabel in 1906 and pursued its increasingly provocative, even violent, campaign for women's rights. In Manchester the cause was advanced by more peaceful means. It was not until 1918 that women over the age of 30 (and men over the age of 21) were allowed to vote. Women had to be married or a member of the Local Government Register. A full century later, after a fundraising campaign, a statue of Emmeline was finally unveiled in Manchester.

WAKE-UP CALLS

The first mill outing (in 1846), from Swinton to Blackpool, demanded a 3 a.m. wake-up call! Afraid of oversleeping, the excursionists engaged two old soldiers to go through the village playing fife and kettle drum to rouse them. Few trippers had seen the sea and the charge of 1/- and 1d for the band seems a real bargain for a lifetime experience. The repeal of the Corn Law in the same year prompted Richard Cobden, a leading figure in the Anti-Corn Law League, to celebrate. He gave a day's wages and an outing to Fleetwood to his workers in the Crosse Hall calico printing works at Chorley. At 6 a.m. a procession of more than a thousand strong accompanied by two brass bands marched to the station to board a train of thirty-nine carriages. They savoured the delights of the seaside, promenading, bathing and eating a huge meal at the Fleetwood Arms. On their return, they were greeted by a huge crowd with another musical march and festivities until 'the night was far spent'.

Fleetwood had also been the venue for 2,384 (exactly?) Sunday school scholars and their teachers on an outing from Preston in 1842. They were met by twenty-seven open carriages at the station and sang hymns for half an hour on the platform at Poulton-le-Fylde on the way. It was a Saturday to avoid profanation of the Sabbath but one Sunday in 1844, Fleetwood greeted a train of thirty-eight carriages, most of them third class, and 1,700 men, women and children. Most were workers and 300 of them sailed to Piel Harbour to visit the ruins of Furness Abbey. Excursions were attended by risks. A boat carrying twenty-one people from the shore to the steamer capsized 'through the thoughtlessness of the passengers' into 'very deep water'[21] but all were rescued. A large number of others forgot the passage of time and were left behind.

Soon Blackpool, Morecambe and Southport were joined to the main railway network by branch lines and attracted the bulk of the tourist trade that developed before comparable connections from London to the south coast. The line to Fleetwood had been opened as early as 1840 and the excursions there could have been the earliest in the country as the line from London to Brighton only opened a year later.

The 'wakes' weeks, when firms closed for their workers to enjoy a communal break, contributed enormously to the economy of the region. Associated excursions grew enormously in scale and complexity. For the day tripper living out of town, schedules demanded both starting and finishing in the early hours. In 1904 thousands of 'excursionists' from the works of Bass, Ratcliffe and Gretton travelled from Burton upon Trent into Liverpool Central Station, on seventeen trains in one day. The ninety-six-page brochure handbook for their employees advertised a huge range of activities and places that could be visited, from beaches to art galleries. You could return late on the same day or extend your holiday to other resorts on the mainland or the Isle of Man. Three spare ships (!) were available for tours in the docks: White Star's *Teutonic* and Cunard's *Ivernia* and *Lucania*. The latter was the joint-largest passenger liner afloat when she entered service in 1893 (the other being her sister ship, *Campania*) and won the Blue Riband on her second voyage.

Las Vegas of the North

Blackpool's phenomenal rise to be the Las Vegas of the north began in the last decade of the nineteenth century. A third pier was added to its repertoire; the tower, great wheel, Empress Ballroom and Empire and Alhambra Theatres were built; the North Shore Promenade was completed; and the South Shore Promenade was widened with its attendant Pleasure Beach. All these would eventually grow into the Golden Mile (actually 1.6 miles) of hotels, boarding houses and amusements, especially the slot machines from which it gets its name. A myriad boarding houses welcomed the cotton mill workers on their annual week's holiday or 'wakes'. Dates were staggered to provide a regular income and source Blackpool's wealth. Boarding rates were cheap then, driven on by fierce competition and the influx of visitors coming by trainloads in profusion. Visitors were attracted by the ever popular donkey rides, Punch and Judy, fortune tellers and the music hall.

Blackpool Tower with Tower Buildings in front, comprising the ballroom, circus and other attractions.

During the twentieth century, Blackpool became bigger, bolder, brasher, more boisterous. This was the essential ingredient of its survival and success: it adapted to the changing times. A pioneering electric tramway system (the first in Britain) was opened in 1885 with electricity drawn from a conduit between the rails by means of a plough. This was replaced by the overhead lines in 1898. Now, retired trams have been sourced from all over the country to run in a miscellany of colours and designs and mingle with the cream and green of Blackpool's own livery. The 518ft Tower bore no comparison with the 906ft Eiffel Tower of 1889 in Paris but looked down on the Great Wheel, which was 220ft high. In 1928, having made a loss for many years, the wheel was taken over by the Tower Company and demolished. In 1990 the new Ferris wheel, a puny 108ft high, was erected on the nearby Central Pier. Still in operation from 1904 is the Pleasure Beach's first major attraction, the 'Captive Flying Machine' or rotary swing ride, designed by the inventor Sir Hiram Maxim (inventor of the First World War machine gun). The beach's first wooden roller coaster opened in 1907 and its successor, 'The Big One', at 213ft high, was the tallest in the world when it was unleashed in 1994. It was reduced to being just the tallest in the land when it was eclipsed by a Japanese attraction two years later. Open-air swimming baths, the largest in the world at the time of opening in 1923, were demolished in 1983 and have been replaced by the ultra-modern Sandcastle Waterpark in the same footprint. The present 6 miles of illuminations started with eight carbon arc lamps that bathed the Promenade in light in 1879, a year before Edison patented his electric light bulb. You can appreciate them from car or tram and the continual kaleidoscope of colour is enjoyed by many annual pilgrims.

The Great Lancashire Golf Boom

A journey along the coast of Lancashire in 1914 would mark not just the end of the Edwardian era but also of the great English golf boom. It would embrace the most concentrated group of links and elite courses in the country. England as a whole was slow to start after the game's birth in Scotland, where there were already nearly twenty clubs before England's second club was formed at Kersal Moor near Manchester. It was formed, unsurprisingly, by two Scotsmen and, again unsurprisingly, by a cotton mill owner and a cotton merchant. It was not until decades later that the first Lancashire course was founded at Blundellsands, Crosby (West Lancs, as it is affectionately called). As with other parts of the country, railways were a catalyst for growth rather than a trigger for an instant start and they certainly helped with the formation of courses as people moved further and further out from Liverpool to settle along the coast. Before the mass advent of the car, most people cycled or walked to the local courses, even the more elite and expensive ones, as here. They were important social institutions and most of them associated with superior residential developments.

A Links Tour by Rail

Although the conflagration was slow in coming, once started this greatest ensemble of links golf courses anywhere spread like wildfire along the Liverpool, Crosby & Southport Railway line (opened fully in 1850). Let us take a journey along the line starting from Liverpool and heading north.

The West Lancashire course is the tenth oldest in the land (1873). It also sported another distinction: a women's club, the first in the county, boasting by far the largest membership in the country in 1914. It had been founded in 1891 but was to be merged with the men after the Second World War. Splendid views over the Mersey Estuary can be enjoyed, including the Wirral, where Open Championships are held at the Royal Liverpool links course at Hoylake in Cheshire. Members of that club founded the West Lancs and so set in motion the chain reaction along the coast.

Take the train along the line straight from tee to tee for the next links courses of the two Formby golf clubs, incorporating a Site of Special Scientific Interest. The Ladies Club has the unique distinction of being the only one left in the country. As with others, men used to be able to join only as associated members, but the passing of the Equalities Act means that they can no longer offer this type of membership as it is deemed to be discriminatory!

Now, at this point, you sidestep to the Formby Hall Golf Club (created since, but not on linksland). Hopping back on the train, you pass the abode of the natterjack toad.

Alight at the next but one station on the line for the Southport and Ainsdale course. The adjoining Royal Birkdale was superior, charging more for membership, and now hosts the Open Championship. The mission of golf had spread along the coast, as the first two captains were ex-West Lancashire.

Sandwiched between the Ainsdale and Birkdale courses is now the tasty filling of the renowned Hillside Golf Club. It moved here from inland pastures in 1925 and has hosted a number of amateur and professional championships.

This fine array of clubs closes with the Hesketh course at the north end of Southport. The neighbouring Municipal course is matched by the Bootle Municipal at the other end of the borough.

As seen from the Hesketh course, cross the estuary of the River Ribble before your next port of call at Fylde for Royal Lytham St Anne's, another Open Championship course, and St Anne's Old Links. This was less exclusive and appealed to shopkeepers and tradesman, like Blackpool North, and maybe Blackpool South, which were to be developed for other purposes in the 1920s.

Despite two world wars and the depression of the 1930s, the survival rate of the 'boom' Lancashire linksland clubs is impressive and their heritage endures.

MEXICO DISASTER

Lancashire has witnessed incalculable shipwrecks but none so tragic as the *Mexico* disaster. The needless loss of life of the lifeboatmen and the impact on their community aroused the sympathy of the whole nation. Even Queen Victoria noted it in her journal as 'terrible and inconceivable'.

The three-masted, iron-hulled ship *Mexico*, sailing from Liverpool for Ecuador in 1886, had battled for four days against gale-force winds in the Irish Sea but was forced back towards Formby Point. She became lodged on one of the sandbanks in the Ribble Estuary. In the darkness of a late evening in December, her distress signals were first seen by the lifeboat station at Southport, and at St Anne's, who fired a rocket to alert their crew. This was also heard at Lytham and runners were sent to assemble the crew there. Within an hour and a half, these two boats had been launched. The Southport boat left half an hour later as shire horses had to pull it 3½ miles along the beach to find the best point to approach the wreck. The Lytham boat, first to reach the *Mexico*, had downed its sails a quarter of a mile from the stricken vessel. As it closed in, a sudden squall broke three of the lifeboat's oars but at 12.30 a.m. a lifeline was thrown to the *Mexico*. The rope broke twice before the crew of twelve were successfully drawn to safety with the captain finally tying the rope round himself and swinging on board. Yet another oar was broken as the lifeboat pulled away.

The Lytham boat passed Ainsdale beach on its way home. There, the onlooking crowd, thinking it was the Southport boat, wondered why it did not come ashore. In reality, when the Southport boat *Eliza Fernley* had reached the *Mexico* half an hour after the rescue, it had capsized as it drew alongside. Two of the crew reached shore alive but dazed and unbeknownst to each other. One of these was discovered by his father (who lost two of his other sons in the disaster). They raised the alarm but resuscitation failed to save others and several bodies were found later.

The *Eliza Fernley* had still not returned. During the search, a lifeboat from Blackpool nearly capsized. The missing boat was found at 1 p.m. that day with all the crew drowned.

The death of twenty-seven crew members for one rescue is the worst in the history of the Royal National Lifeboat Institution. The effect on the local communities was devastating. The loss of young men, many closely related, affected some families catastrophically. A national fund was set up to which Queen Victoria contributed £100. The German Kaiser generously donated £250 in appreciation of the sacrifice that the crews had suffered to save the lives of the German captain and others on board the *Mexico*. The total raised more than £30,000.

Memorials were raised near all the lifeboat stations and they have survived in good condition to this day. The Lytham St Anne's lifeboat station, run by the RNLI, operates two lifeboats on separate sites. The Southport lifeboat station, run by the Southport Offshore Rescue Trust, has been replaced with a modern building and equipment.

A few miles down the coast at Formby, all that remains of the first lifeboat station in Britain (and possibly in the world) is a sandstone plinth and some fragmented brickwork half-covered by sand. First documented in 1776, it also had its own disaster in 1836 when the lifeboat went down with all five hands. Between them they left behind four widows and thirty-eight children. The widows received a life pension of 2*s* a week (a bare subsistence allowance). One widow, left pregnant with thirteen children, lived another sixty-two years, dying at 104 years old as recorded on her tombstone in St Peter's Church graveyard in Formby.

9

DECLINE AND RENEWAL

MANCHESTER VS LIVERPOOL

The Manchester Ship Canal was one of the greatest engineering achievements of the Victorian era. It was also a gamechanger in the rivalry between Liverpool and Manchester on the industrial field. The difficulties and costs of freight traffic between the two cities had been greatly reduced by the construction of the Liverpool & Manchester Railway. However, the advantages that it brought were heavily in favour of Liverpool merchants. They profited in particular from the increasing volume of imports and exports, especially cotton, flowing through the port, and on from there by rail, and were able to dictate prices. Further aggravation was felt by Manchester merchants when Oldham spinners bought cotton on the Continent, imported it through Hull and transported it by rail across the Pennines more cheaply than via Liverpool. Half the cost of exporting cotton goods to India was absorbed by Liverpool's railway and dock charges.

In 1882 a historic meeting was held in the Didsbury home of Daniel Atkinson, head of an engineering business in Dukinfield, Manchester. Fifty-five merchants and thirteen representatives of large Lancashire cotton towns had been invited to consider plans for a canal that would bring ocean-going ships straight through to a major international port in the city. The cost and engineering prospects were formidable. Manchester Corporation loaned one third of the capital, and the largest number of shareholders in a private company at the time (39,000) contributed the rest. The construction to the depth of the Suez Canal, essential for a direct route to India, excited the admiration and interest of contemporaries. Modern techniques reduced dependence on navvies as the heaviest work was carried out by seventy-five steam excavators, 124 steam cranes and seven earth dredgers working from the hank. The scale of some of the engineering work was prodigious and prompted ingenious technological solutions: the triple locks at the entrance, for example, and the unique swing bridge that carried the Bridgewater Canal over it. The railway line from Warrington through Lymm was forced to climb 75ft on an embankment to clear the canal on the Latchford Viaduct. The ambition did not stop with the canal itself. Eight docks were built at Manchester with over 6 miles of quays. Four were on the site of the Pomona Botanical Gardens and Zoo, mostly in the borough of Stretford. Three were wholly in the borough of Salford and were joined by the largest dock, occupying the site of the old racecourse opened by King Edward VII in 1906. All these were serviced by a canal railway system with over 230 miles of track and seventy-five locomotives. This infrastructure was crucial during the Second World War. Following the nationalisation of the main line network in 1948, it became the largest private network of lines in the country.

A 1920s advertisement proclaimed: 'ONE STRIDE! Manchester lies at the heart of the world's most closely packed population – the world's biggest market. Imports consigned direct to the port. Reach it in one stride!' Trafford Park, originally the ancestral home of the de Trafford family and adjacent to the Salford Docks, developed as the first industrial estate in the world. Most notably, the Co-operative Wholesale Society food-packing plant and flour mill were constructed, and further on at Irlam, a soap and candle works. Such household names as Ford produced its Model T; Westinghouse its turbines and generators; followed by Rank Hovis McDougall, British Alizarine Co. in the 1920s (later part of ICI), Jacobs of cream cracker fame and the soap works of Proctor & Gamble. All the factories were connected to the railway network. Kellogg's new factory of 1938 boosted the import of foodstuffs.

However, the glory of the Manchester Ship Canal was short-lived. Modern container ships were too large for the canal. One hundred years after its construction all was changed and much had disappeared. The Barton Swing Bridge is still admired but hardly used. The Latchford Viaduct remained long after it was closed. The canal company refused to close the canal for the nine days needed for its demolition. Such an effort to construct and toil to demolish! The Salford Docks now host visitors to the Museum of War together with the Lowry theatre and gallery complex and its associated residential, commercial and retail accommodation.

Trade through Liverpool was saved by the construction of the Royal Seaforth container dock but the redundant docks, as at Manchester, are being converted for leisure purposes. In the south, the docks have all been closed but now contain new and converted accommodation, ranging from the Inland Revenue to the Royal Liverpool Yacht Club. In the north, hotels abound, and the redevelopment has included a new stadium for Everton Football Club. At the centre, the Albert Dock has been revitalised as a major tourist attraction, accompanied by the Museum of Liverpool and the Arena conference centre.

TITANIC LIVERPOOL

Titanic was built in Belfast and sailed from Southampton on her fateful last voyage, but Liverpool was more closely connected with her than any other city. The headquarters of the White Star Line, who owned her, stood on the waterfront. It looked like New Scotland Yard in London and was designed by the same architect. The chairman lived in a grand mansion just along the coast on the banks of the Mersey, from where he could observe his passing ships. Close by was the captain's terraced residence and the second officer's semi-detached house. The captain went down with his ship but the chairman had stepped into a spare place in a lifeboat at the last minute. The second officer escaped, miraculously, and was picked up by the rescuing ship *Carpathia*, whose captain lived just round the corner from where he lived. Not so the chief engineer and the chief steward, also living near, and eighty-five of the 115 'Liverpool connected' crew and thirteen of the seventeen passengers with strong Liverpool connections. These were out of a total of 892 crew and 1,317 passengers.

When *Titanic* sank, Liverpool was at the height of its Edwardian maritime prosperity. Yet another of its early docks, George's, had become redundant but new ones had been added, culminating in the huge Gladstone Dock in 1927. The entrance lock, it was boasted, was capable of taking the largest liner ever built, or likely to be built (before the advent of the latest cruise ships!). George's Dock was filled in and 'graced' with three buildings of outstanding quality, worthy of World Heritage status until they were deprived of the honour by overshadowing high-rise blocks. The 'Three Graces' were, in order of construction: the Liver Building, a steel-framed skyscraper of its time, adorned with liver birds, emblems of Liverpool, the Mersey Docks and Harbour Board Building, and the Cunard Building. The palatial architecture and ornamentation of this expressed eloquently the firm's domination of the Atlantic passenger trade that had brought so much wealth into the city. However, at that very time, the sailings of the largest liners had been transferred to Southampton. Within fifty years, passengers crossing the Atlantic by boat had all but disappeared.

The name *Titanic* lives on in Liverpool. The largest warehouse in the port was constructed for tobacco, one of the largest brick buildings in the world (27 million bricks). It is being converted into 500 apartments with an associated Titanic Hotel.

WAR AND PEACE

At the outbreak of the First World War, the industrial and commercial power of Lancashire seemed unassailable. But there were signs, maybe with hindsight, of weaknesses. Foreign competition, especially in cotton, intensified successfully as Britain concentrated industrial output on arms production. Resources were not available for investment in outdated infrastructure. Social stability, especially in decaying inner cities, was subjected to stress and dismemberment. Men and women performed new roles.

Lancashire took the lead in recruitment for the army. Following a suggestion that men might be more likely to volunteer for service alongside friends and colleagues, a battalion of 1,600 soldiers was raised in London. Lord Derby took up the idea and obtained permission from Lord Kitchener to recruit with a similar campaign. Speaking to an initial battalion of Liverpudlians, he said, 'This should be a battalion of pals.' The name stuck. Within the next few days three more battalions were raised to form the 17th, 18th, 19th and 20th Battalions of the King's Regiment (Liverpool). When Lord Kitchener then promoted the idea throughout the country, more than fifty towns raised Pals Battalions. Manchester alone raised four immediately, then another four and, three months later, another four. The results were at first encouraging and then devastating. When the Accrington Pals were ordered to attack on the opening day of the 1916 Somme Offensive, 584 out of the battalion of 700 were killed, wounded or missing, most of them within the space of twenty minutes. The brother of one of those killed said that there was scarcely a street in Accrington that did not have the blinds drawn and the bell at Christ Church tolled all day. Out of a total population of about 14,000, the First World War names recorded on the memorial amount to 865. This contrasts with only 173 on a wall that was added to commemorate those who died in the Second World War.

Only rarely are women and children honoured by a dedication on a war memorial. Rawtenstall is special. Here, they are implied by the wording: 'Tribute of Honour/To the Men Who/ Made the Supreme Sacrifice/To the Men Who Came Back/ And to Those Who Worked at Home/To Win Safety for the Empire/ 1914–1918'. The cenotaph was unveiled by a former suffragette in 1929, eleven years after the close of the war, and its inclusivity is remarkable for its time. All three forces, Army, Navy and Air Force, are portrayed by statues – and the medical corps, too. Other figures represent women on service in the Land Army, Forestry Service, Royal Naval Service and Army Auxiliary Corps. A nurse, munitions worker and woman with child are also shown. Civilians appear as labourers and a fisherman, special constable, postman, railwayman and mechanic.

Lancashire has more outstanding war memorials, as listed and judged by Historic England to be of Grade I and Grade II* standard, than any other region in the country. It seems that Lancastrians were, for some reason, more motivated to raise money generously and engage the best architect, as Liverpool and Accrington did, or wait until the best materials were available, as in Southport. Women's skills were diverted to manufacturing military equipment. In peacetime, Waring & Gillow, based in Lancaster, produced high-quality furniture for some of the wealthiest people in the country. In Lancashire alone, they supplied fittings, fixtures and furniture in Lancaster Town Hall, the stalls in the Anglican cathedral in Liverpool and the panelling in Stretford Town Hall, Greater Manchester. The firm advertised their contribution to the war effort with a publicity photograph. Young girls were among those pictured in their workshop assembling ammunition cases. It exhibited the workers' patriotism in volunteering their services and the good conditions in which they worked.

Lancashire had at least four major locomotive manufacturers: Gorton 'Tank' and Beyer Peacock in Manchester, the Vulcan Foundry in Newton le Willows and the Lancashire & Yorkshire

Railway works at Horwich. In addition, the company of Dick, Kerr in Preston manufactured tramcars as well as locomotives. There, women were pictured assembling and painting seaplane wings in 1918 at the end of the First World War. Following informal lunch and tea break football matches, played against the apprentices, the famous Dick, Kerr Ladies FC was founded in 1917. Their star player was Lily Parr, scouted by the team at the age of 14. She went on to play for St Helens Ladies, where she had been born, once in front of a crowd of 53,000 at Everton's Goodison Park. This popularity, which threatened the men's game, led to the Football Association banning women members and their playing on men's grounds (for fifty years!). She has now been belatedly honoured by a statue in the National Football Museum in Manchester.

DECLINE AND FALL OF THE COTTON EMPIRE

The American Civil War was a turning point for Lancashire cotton. This led to specialisation and innovation in Oldham, Blackburn, Burnley and Rochdale. The self-acting mule was improved to increase its speed of operation and versatility. The Edwardian era was, for Lancashire's cotton towns, truly an *Indian* summer. Before the First World War, the prosperity of Lancashire cotton towns was bound up with exports to India. Eighty per cent of the production went for export (30 per cent to India), reversing what had been the case a century before. This link was to have far-reaching consequences half a century later. But now, in 1913, over 65 per cent of the world's cotton was the produce of Lancashire's looms. In Bolton, six-sevenths of its industrial output went abroad, two-fifths of this to India. Bolton was thus strongly 'imperially minded'. In China there was fierce competition with the United States, although British exporters retained the advantage in finer shirts and sheets.

After the war the British Empire was at its height. A fifth of the world population owed allegiance to King George V and Liverpool was the fourth busiest port in the world. Only Hong Kong, London and New York surpassed it. Lancashire had weathered the storm but lost its export market of cotton, particularly of the cheaper quality, to India, China, Japan and Hong Kong. Ironically, much of their equipment had been manufactured in Britain. In the 1920s Britain was overtaken as the largest producer of cotton cloth by the United States, which supplied most of Britain's import of the material, to be overtaken by Japan in the 1930s. India had contributed a war loan and the government decided on a tariff on goods to India to repay it. In retaliation, Gandhi boycotted Lancashire goods.

By 1939 exports to India had suffered a catastrophic decline. Unemployment in Lancashire had peaked overall at 38.5 per cent in 1931. Pockets in the weaving belt rose to 47.9 per cent. Lobbying by the Manchester Chamber of Commerce and Lord Derby (dubbed the King of Lancashire for championing the industry) were to no avail. Frantic efforts were made to advertise

In 1931 Corder Catchpool, Quaker manager of the Spring Vale Garden Village, invited Gandhi to Lancashire in the hope that the sight of the workers' poverty would induce him to lift his boycott. Here, he is visiting India (!) Cotton Mill in Darwen.

home-produced cotton. A 'Cotton Queen' competition was held with the winner being crowned in regal style at Blackpool and then touring the county, feted as she went.

Employers sought to make production more competitive by wage reductions and more efficient working practices. Negotiations on one of these, the 'more looms' issue, developed into the greatest and most bitter industrial conflict of the 1930s. By tradition, four looms were worked by one weaver, who was responsible for replacing the weft in the shuttle when it ran out. The employers bargained for a weaver to manage twice the number of looms, but the unions objected that the increased pay was not enough for a man to support a wife staying at home. Experiments were even carried out with an automatic replacement that would enable one weaver to manage twenty-four or even forty looms but they proved that the cost of installing this would be prohibitively expensive. After protracted and rancorous negotiations, a compromise was reached but, even then, adopted in some areas and not in others.

Paid holidays was another issue. From the end of the nineteenth century, many working-class families took an annual holiday at the seaside. This was helped by the highly developed railway links and use of charabancs, which had led in turn to the attraction of improved facilities and amenities in the seaside resorts. It was associated with the Wakes weeks, when a mass exodus of workers left the mills free for essential maintenance. Families could afford this through savings clubs, charities and other organisations of mutual help. However, there were others who could not benefit from it and the unions argued for paid holidays to enable them to enjoy the holidays with the extra expenses involved. As a ditty of the time points out:

> There's the grocery bill, and clubman's arrears
> We mun' settle the rent and the landlady's fears
> And when mother has settled her debts wi' them all
> Bought Bertie a jacket and Alice a shawl

She looks in her purse – and alack and alas –
There's just a bob left from the 'holiday' brass.

The cotton workers' unions argued that even in the industry itself some operatives received holiday pay, and certainly office staff did. Both sides pointed out that it would lead to the increased productivity of a 'contented and healthy worker'. Although the matter had been raised soon after the First World War, the employers argued that with the depressed state of the economy they could not afford it and the concession was not finally resolved until 1939. By then, cloth exports had plummeted to less than a fifth of the 1913 level and the war broke out.

During the Second World War imports of raw cotton ceased. Factories came under government control and were used for munitions. Barnoldswick, for example, produced and later designed aero engines for Rolls-Royce. Weaving was re-established in the early 1950s, but there was a lack of machinery and skills, and India was exporting to Britain! Protection for the industry was not achieved until 1972 but it was too late. The pressure of cotton goods being produced more cheaply abroad forced an inevitable surrender and the last mill, Bancroft Shed, closed in 1978.

The Road to Wigan Pier

How the legendary Wigan 'pier' originated is debatable. Most likely, an excursion train bound for Southport was passing through the town. It stopped where a trestle carried a mineral line over the canal. 'Where on earth are we?' by one passenger was answered by a witty 'Wigan Pier!' The laugh was that industrial Wigan was far from the sea and no way likely to rival Southport's grand pier. George Formby picked up the joke and it was immortalised by him and others far and wide, even in Wigan's music hall.

George Orwell, Old Etonian and London-based journalist, arrived in Wigan in 1936, and recorded his encounters in his book *The Road to Wigan Pier* (Penguin 1986). He had been sent by a publisher to reveal to the public at large the miserable state of the northern working class in a time of depression. It was a revelation to Orwell himself. His first encounter with reality was a boarding house, where he lodged in an ex-drawing room with four beds. He could only spread his 6ft 2½in frame when his neighbour departed for the pits at 5 a.m. to work 'on top' as a mechanic at a coal pit. Opposite was a Scottish miner, injured when a huge stone had pinned him to the ground for a couple of hours. He had received compensation of £500 and lay in bed for most of the day. The other, double, bed was occupied by a string of commercial travellers, newspaper canvassers and hire purchase touts. The windows were tight shut and the room 'stank like a ferret's cage'. The meals were 'uniformly disgusting': for breakfast, two rashers of bacon, a pale fried egg and bread and butter, cut overnight with dirty thumb marks on it; for dinner, a tinned threepenny steak pudding with boiled potatoes and rice pudding; for tea, bread and butter with stale sweet cakes; for supper, 'pale, flabby' Lancashire cheese and biscuits.

When he inspected the mines, Orwell was at severe disadvantage in getting his gangly frame to the coal face. To reach it, you might have to crouch or crawl 3 miles from the base of the lift shaft. Your head might be protected by a helmet, but your back would scrape against the tunnel ceiling. Miners developed 'buttons down the back', a permanent scab on each vertebra. This return journey, and the one from the pit back home, was added to the day's work. The 'fillers' worked seven and a half hours at a stretch digging out the coal, theoretically without a break, but they might snatch a quarter of an hour to consume a hunk of bread, dripping and a bottle of cold tea. Orwell likened conditions at the coal face to hell: heat, noise, confusion, darkness, foul air and unbearably cramped space. The air was black with asphyxiating coal dust that would eventually poison the lungs. The strain on the muscles was unremitting, at times unbearable and intense. There was constant danger: descent in the cage down the shaft, trucks hauling the coal away, gas explosions, flying debris set off by explosives to loosen the seams of coal and rockfalls – if you were unlucky, on top or behind you.

Orwell stayed in the home of a 15-year-old boy who was on night shift. The boy left home at nine at night and returned home at eight in the morning. After breakfast, he slept until six in the evening, leaving him barely four hours for any sort of recreation. His prospect in life, besides injury or an early death, might include lung or eye disease. A disability pension might compensate but would be determined by the solvency of the colliery company. He would be expected to be grateful for this, and his status was low. But he was absolutely essential for the well-being of his 'superiors', for powering the cotton industry on which depended Lancashire's industrial might and for the prosperity of the population as a whole.

Wigan has a lot to be proud of. Besides coal and cotton, it was at one time the most important centre for bell making in the north. The town was in the County of Lancashire for centuries until 1974, when it was absorbed into Greater Manchester, and many Wiganers consider themselves Lancastrians to this day. The lake and pavilion of Mesnes (pronounced mains) are set in a 30-acre park in the town centre. The Mesnes, part of the former manorial demesnes land, and the site of two collieries, was obtained by Wigan Corporation in the 1870s. The old Rugby League stadium was embedded in the local community and marked by its name, Central Park. Strong support came from out of town too and the ground once held 36,895 spectators in a World Club Championship match. Wigan Rugby League Club, dating from the 1870s, claims to be the most successful club rugby league team in the world. Along with neighbouring arch-rivals St Helens and Leigh, it formed the Lancastrian stronghold for the Rugby League code. A new stadium completed in 1999 is shared with Wigan Athletic Football Club, where it now plays as Wigan Warriors.

Eric Blair (George Orwell was a pseudonym) died soon after he retired in 1948 to the remote island of Jura to write his prophetic and prophesying work *Nineteen Eighty Four* (1984). In it he stoutly maintained his belief in the principle of freedom of speech and the evils of the totalitarian state. Winston, the hero of the work, reflects the same ideals as his contemporary, Winston Churchill.

BOOTLE BLITZ

Bootle, for its size, suffered more damage during the Second World War than any other area in the country. It was the target of the Luftwaffe because of the critical role Merseyside Docks played in the Battle of the Atlantic to save the country from starvation. Most of the Liverpool docks lay alongside Bootle, and were part of it, so the borough suffered both direct and collateral damage from bombing. The greatest damage was caused when SS *Malakand* caught fire in Huskisson Dock in 1941. The ship was carrying 1,000 tons of explosives and when ignited the blast propelled debris 2½ miles distant. Before the outbreak of war, Bootle's population totalled 76,000, living in 17,000 houses. By the end of the war, the people had been subjected to 502 air-raid warnings, 460 people had been killed and 1,881 injured; 2,043 houses had been totally destroyed and only forty escaped damage altogether. At the height of the May 1941 Blitz, which lasted for eight days, 20,000 people were made homeless (many of the 13,000 evacuated at the outbreak of the war had returned); finally, fewer than 10,000 men and women stayed in town during the night, although 30,000 lived and worked there during the day. Their heroism ensured not only that vital supplies came into the country but also that destroyers left base there to sink enemy submarines.

Johnnie Walker

Hanging in the council chamber of Bootle Town Hall are the wind-torn flags of Captain 'Johnnie' Walker's ships. Born Frederic John Walker, he was popularly known by the brand of whisky. His home, 'Flotilla House', on the corner of Trinity Road and Pembroke Road, displays a plaque recording his decorations: CB (Companion of the Order of the Bath) and DSO (Distinguished Service Order) with three bars. He was recognised as being supremely instrumental, among British and Allied officers, for winning the Allied victory of the Battle of the Atlantic, one of the most important campaigns of the war. Through his innovative methods, his destroyer sank more U-boats during the Battle of the Atlantic than any other. He claimed the sinking of six U-boats in one patrol alone. One of the most valuable consignments to cross the Atlantic was a convoy of gold, conveying Britain's gold reserves to Canada during the Second World War. It was stowed secretly in Martin's Bank Headquarters building in Liverpool before being transferred at night for shipment to a heavily armoured convoy.

Johnnie Walker suffered a stroke attributed to overwork and exhaustion on 7 July 1944. He died two days later.

The Road from Wigan Pier

Wigan Pier was brought to life for a brief and glorious period in 1982. A superior warehouse was converted into a museum of Victorian life and revived the name. It had been built in the late nineteenth century and was distinguished by its clock tower and canopy to protect cargoes and workers loading barges. Visitors were enlightened by a Victorian classroom, a colliery disaster and working textile machinery. But Wigan could not shake off its industrial image. The attractive and entertaining venture closed in the depression of 2007.

Decline and Renewal

Lancashire revived! The Leeds & Liverpool canal approaching Wigan Pier with reflections past and present.

Since the depression of the 1930s, times have changed. The collieries and cotton mills have closed, the slag heaps have been landscaped and beautified. No more do the 'coal searchers' pictured in Orwell's work pick over the slag for scraps of fuel, thrown away by collieres. There is still deprevation to be found – a modern investigator[22] met a girl who had been abused for three years by her grandfather. She was waiting in a dirty hostel in Manchester for transfer to a mother and baby unit in Birmingham. But at least she had a room of her own with a sink, a bed and a wardrobe.

However, there are great success stories from Orwell's era, too. A miner, who met Orwell in 1936, had left school at 14 and gone straight down the mines. His son grew up in houses with three to a room, outside toilets and no running water. He received free school meals during the war, then won a scholarship to Wigan Grammar School, graduated in law at Oxford and was called to the bar. His children qualified as solicitors and his grandchildren were heading for university. His father, when he met Orwell, was out of work. He had been banned from the pits for organising strikes and tainted by being a communist. He was reinstated during the war as they needed miners, then became union organiser, engaged in the overuse of pit props and schemes to ratchet up wages.

The county suffered grievously during and after the Miners' Strike in 1984. The year before there had been unrest and a sign of the troubles to come. The Parkside Pit in Newton-le-Willows, with twenty-five years of coal reserves and 800 workers, was modern, efficient and as clean as could be. The Lancashire Women Against Pit Closures made national news by setting up a camp in the pit. After four days down below, they came up, leaving it tidy of course. It was the last pit to close in the Lancashire coalfield in 1993, to be replaced by new hills formed from the slag heaps and by 'flashes' (lakes) created from the subsidence. By that time, at Astley Green Colliery near Leigh, the winding house and 98ft-high headstock still stood (though in ruinous condition) as 'a noble and mournful monument to a vast industry' (Pevsner, architectural authority). Pit production had begun in 1912, and the colliery was modernised when nationalisation came in 1947, but it closed in 1970. The two large wheels and a small wheel at the top of the headstock have survived and the winding house has now been restored. It has reopened as the only Lancashire coal mining museum, with the largest steam winding engine used on the coalfield once again in working order. At Parkside, plans to redevelop the colliery into an industrial estate and logistics hub have been approved.

Early this century ex-miners' membership of the Astley and Tyldesley Miners' Welfare Club shrunk to ten. Couples from Liverpool and Manchester living in the new housing estates made up the rest. The chairman had suffered a crippling accident and the National Coal Board let him recover on full pay for eighteen months. When he returned to work, they gave him the holiday that had accrued and finally a handsome pay-off. Wigan's biggest employers were the council, the national health trust, the bus company, and food manufacturing. Now, a factory is far safer than a mine, much less stressful and physically punishing, but there is a transient, maybe overseas, Asian or eastern European, workforce. Supermarkets offer good working conditions and training and career opportunities. But casual and changing contracts remind you of the infamous Liverpool dockers system of hiring fresh workers each day. Lucky were those who caught the eye of the boss at the right time! As time passed, for young people under 30 wishing for a long-term job, the best chance was in the police or charities.

The old terrace housing that Orwell experienced was destroyed by a dual carriageway and the post-war fetish for tower blocks. The theory was that a new, vertical community would grow in green spaces. In fact, the old camaraderie of the terrace streets with no corners or hideaways was destroyed. Crime prospered in lift shafts and anonymous balconies. Drugs, with their insidious network, replaced the old but open evils of alcohol. When the tower blocks themselves were replaced by low-rise housing on estates on the outskirts of the town, a jumble of people from distant communities found no immediate feeling for each other but positive antagonism. Such tower blocks as survived suffered from lack of care and maintenance, beset by damp and the dangers of cladding. Cities all over the land experienced the same fate. Many of the mills have been repurposed for storage, shopping or other industrial uses, including textiles such as carpets, soft furnishings or imported fabrics. In Burnley, with its tradition of engineering from earlier spinning and weaving equipment, new aero opportunities have sprung up. Integration has been helped by restructuring of education and vocational courses initiated by universities.

In many parts of Lancashire, the greatest change in population has been the growth of the Asian population and hence of

Muslims. In fact, the latest census shows that Blackburn with Darwen has one of the highest proportions of Muslim population (35 per cent) in the country, second only to a London borough. In Blackburn, the growth greatly expanded in the late 1960s and through the '70s, attracted by the strong textile tradition and the opportunities for a comparatively better life and better-paid employment. Unfortunately, the decline in the cotton industry has increased the unemployment figures. The Asian population has tended to congregate in close-knit areas in owner-occupied housing and their younger than average age has increased their proportion of the population. Over a forty-year period, the skyline has been changed by the construction of twenty-nine mosques and many independent Muslim schools have been opened. Eating habits have been transformed and Blackburn has the widest choice of any in the country.

A partnership encouraged by Prince (now King) Charles and implemented in 1989 regenerated the town and as the smallest borough in the country it benefited enormously from city challenge schemes in the 1990s. Its independence and unity were strengthened by the restoration of services that it had surrendered to the Lancashire County Council in the local council reorganisation of 1974. However, while many middle-aged people have moved elsewhere for better employment, the higher than national average age of the younger unemployed has been cause for concern. Its change from a small country town 250 years ago to new patterns of industrialisation, then boom town, followed by malaise and struggle for revival is typical for much of the county.

In Wigan, as in the other industrial towns in Lancashire, the end of the country's economic dependence on coal has resulted in cleaner air through the closure of mines, alternative forms of power in factories and homes, and the end of steam locomotion on the railways. This has been accompanied by the reclamation of vast areas of polluted and degraded land around towns. Public, private and voluntary sectors have worked together towards a common goal. During the last two centuries, riots have all too often seemed to be futile protests. In the early 1980s, ironically spanning the year of Orwell's *1984*, the Toxteth Riots in Liverpool resulted in a partnership that revitalised the centre of the city. Coincidentally, in 1985, emerged a world first: the Mersey Basin Campaign. This twenty-five-year government-backed movement aimed to create a cleaner environment across the whole Greater Manchester Region. Awarded the first international River Prize in 1999, it left the river system and waterside purer than at any time since the Industrial Revolution and it continues under the aegis of the Mersey Rivers Trust.

Another first, a stretch of motorway to form the Preston Bypass was opened in 1958 and has now been expanded to all quarters of the county and beyond. The Lancashire network has created prosperity and pleasure in business and leisure activity. Topflight football clubs in Blackburn, Liverpool and Manchester, and record-breaking Wigan Rugby League play in new stadia. But the Northern Powerhouse has yet to be finalised and HS2 terminates at Birmingham.

Such has been the Rocky Road *from* Wigan Pier.

ENDNOTES

1. See formby-footprints.co.uk, as well as book publications by Gordon Roberts.
2. Morgan, Philip, *Domesday Book Cheshire* (including Lancashire) (Phillimore, Chichester, 1978) and Gray, Andrew E.P., *The Domesday record of the land between Ribble and Mersey* (HSLC Transactions vol 39, 1889).
3. Wikipedia: Geoffrey H. White, 'The First House of Bellême', Transactions of the Royal Historical Society, Fourth Series, Vol. 22 (1940), p. 87.
4. Morgan, Philip, *Domesday Book Cheshire* (including Lancashire) (Phillimore, Chichester, 1978).
5. *Ibid.*
6. *Ibid.*
7. France, R Sharpe *A history of Plague in Lancashire Part 1* (HSLC Transactions vol 90 1938).
8. *Ibid.*
9. From the minutes of Liverpool Common Council, 2 April 1777, quoted in Yorke, B. and R., *Britain's First Lifeboat Station, Formby, 1776 – 1918*.
10. Duggan, Mona, *Sugar for the House: a History of Early Sugar Refining in North West England*, (Fonthilll Media, 2013).
11. According to Bank of England Inflation Calculator at the time of writing.
12. Rev. Engelbert Horley, M.A,'The Mock Corporation of Sephton Part I (1881).
13. Quoted in Aspin C, Lancashire, The First Industrial Society, 1750–1850, (Helmshore Local History Society, 1969).
14. *Ibid.*
15. Harrison, Frederic, 'Diary of a visit to Lancashire during the cotton famine', 1863 (London School of Economics and Political science).
16. *The Moral Reformer* as quoted in Aspin C, *The First Industrial Society*, p. 61
17. Aspin, C., *The First Industrial Society: Lancashire, 1750–1850, (Helmshore Local History Society, 1969)*.
18. Harrison, Frederic, 'Diary of a visit to Lancashire during the cotton famine', 1863 (London School of Economics and Political science).
19. Recorded in the Manchester Corporation Minutes.
20. Hyndman, H.M. *Further Reminiscences* (London, 1912).
21. *Preston Chronicle*, 10 August 1844, quoted in Aspin. Excursion on Sunday preceding 4 August.
22. Armstrong, Stephen The Road to Wigan Pier Revisited (Constable, 2012).

BIBLIOGRAPHY

Note: HSLC = Historical Society of Lancashire and Cheshire

Armstrong, R.G., 'The Rise of Morecambe 1820–1862' (HSLC *Transactions*, Vol. 100, 1948).

Armstrong, Stephen, *The Road to Wigan Pier Revisited* (Constable, 2012).

Ashmore, Owen, 'The Diary of James Garnett, of Low Moor, Clitheroe' (HLSC *Transactions* vols 121 [1969 & 123, 1971]).

Aspin, C., *The First Industrial Society: Lancashire, 1750-1850*, (Helmshore Local History Society, 1969).

Baines, *A History of the County of Lancaster:*, ed. William Farrer and J. Brownbill (London, 1907) via British History Online, www.british-history.ac.uk/vch/lancs.

Barker, T.C., 'The Sankey Navigation' (HLSC Transactions, Vol. 100, 1948).

Blackburn Corporation, *Blackburn Centenary Souvenir* (Blackburn Corporation, 1951).

Blundell, Nicholas, *Blundell's Diary from 1702 to 1728* (Crosby Records, 1895).

Blundell, William, *A Cavalier's Note Book* (Longmans, Green & Co., 1880).

Bradshaw, *Bradshaw's Descriptive Railway Hand-book of Great Britain and Ireland* (Old House Books & Maps, 2012).

Bradshaw, *Bradshaw's General Monthly Railway and Steam Navigation Guide for Great Britain and Ireland March 1850* (P. Kay, Teignmouth, *c.* 2012).

Brazendale, David, *Lancashire's Historic Halls* (Carnegie, 2005).

Bryant, Max, *The Museum by the Park: 14 Queen Anne's Gate from Charles Townley to Axel Johnson* (Paul Holberton Publishing, 2017).

Bullock, Derek John, 'The Road from Wigan Pier' (*Pastforward*, Wigan Council, 2022).

Caroe, W.D., *Sefton: a descriptive and historical account with records of the Mock Corporation* (Longmans, Green, and Co., 1893).

Clayton, Marjorie, *A Blackburn Childhood in Wartime* (Landy Publishing, 2000).

Cobb, M.H., *The Railways of Britain: A Historical Atlas* (Ian Alan Publishing, 2003).

Coghlan, Francis, *The Iron Road Book and Railway Companion from London to Liverpool and Manchester* (E. & W. Books, 1970).

De Quincey, Thomas, *Confessions of an English Opium-Eater* (Oxford University Press, 1944).

Duggan, Mona, *Sugar for the House: a History of Early Sugar Refining in North West England* (Fonthilll Media, 2013).

Dutton, H.I. & King, J.E., 'A Fallacy, a Delusion and Snare: arbitration and conciliation in the Preston strike 1853–4' (HSLC *Transactions*, Vol. 131, 1982).

Eckersley, Yvonne, 'Leigh's Poor Law Union 1837–1848' (*Pastforward*, Wigan Council, 2021).

Eckersley, Yvonne, 'Keeping the Peace: Miners, Magistrates and Military in the Wigan District during the 1881 Colliers' Strike' *(Pastforward*, Wigan Council, 2022).

Ewing, Thor, 'Understanding the Heysham Hogback: a tenth century sculpted monument and its context' (HSLC *Transactions*, Vol. 152, 2003).

Ferneyhough, Frank, *Liverpool and Manchester Railway 1830–1980* (Book Club Associates, 1980).

Fishwick, Henry, 'Lancashire in the Time of Charles II' (HSLC *Transactions*, Vol. 33, 1880).

France, R. Sharpe, 'A History of Plague in Lancashire Part 1' (HSLC *Transactions*, Vol. 90, 1938).

Gaskell, Elizabeth, *Mary Barton* (Penguin Books, 2003).

Gibson, A. Craig, 'The Last Popular Risings in the Lancashire Lake Country' (HSLC *Transactions*, Vol. 21, 1868).

Gooderson, P.J., *A History of Lancashire* (Batsford, 1980).

Gray, Andrew E.P., 'The Domesday Record of the Land between Ribble and Mersey' (HSLC *Transactions*, Vol. 39, 1889).

Gray, Edward, *Manchester Ship Canal* (Sutton Publishing, 1997).

Gray, Ted, *A Hundred Years of the Manchester Ship Canal* (Aurora Publishing, 1993).

Hair, P.E.H., 'The Lancashire Collier Girl, 1795' (HSLC *Transactions*, Vol. 120, 1968).

Hale, W.G., & Coney, Audrey, *Martin Mere Lancashire's Lost Lake* (Liverpool University Press, 2008).

Hall, Nigel, 'The Liverpool Cotton Market: Britain's first futures market' (HSLC *Transactions*, Vol. 149, 2000).

Hallam, John, *The Surviving Past: Archaeological finds and excavations in Central Lancashire* (Countryside Publications, 1977).

Bibliography

Harding, Stephen, *Viking Mersey: Scandinavian Wirral, West Lancashire and Chester* (Countyvise, 2002).

Harris, S.A., 'Sarah Clayton's Letter and John Wood of Bath' (HLSC *Transactions*, Vol. 100, 1948).

Harrison, Frederic, 'Diary of a visit to Lancashire during the cotton famine', 1863 (London School of Economics and Political science).

Hearn, David, *The Slave Streets of Liverpool* (The Dusty Teapot Company, 2020).

Hodgkiss, W.J., 'Senley Green Grammar School, Ashton in Makerfield' (HSLC *Transactions*, Vol. 104, 1952).

Hollinghurst, Hugh, *John Foster and Sons, Kings of Georgian Liverpool* (Liverpool History Society, 2009).

Hollinghurst, Hugh, *Little Crosby Historic Village* (Crosby Hall Educational Trust, 2016).

Horley, M.A, Rev. Engelbert, 'The Mock Corporation of Sephton Part I (1881).

Hoult, James, 'Travelling Post' (HSLC *Transactions*, Vol. 72, 1920).

Hunt, David, *A History of Preston* (Carnegie Press, 2009).

Hyndman, H.M, *Further Reminiscences*, London 1912

Jones, S.G., 'The Lancashire Cotton Industry and the Development of Paid Holidays in the nineteen-thirties' (HSLC *Transactions*, Vol. 135, 1986).

Kelly, Michael, *The Life and Times of Kitty Wilkinson* (Countyvise, 2000).

Kidd, Alan, *Manchester, a History* (Carnegie Publishing, 1993).

Lewis, Brian, *Life in a Cotton Town: Blackburn 1818–1848* (Carnegie Press, 1985).

Little, L., 'The Duke's Dock in Liverpool' (HSLC *Transactions*, Vol. 133, 1984).

McCready, H.W., 'Elizabeth Gaskell and the Cotton Famine in Manchester: some unpublished letters' (HSLC *Transactions*, Vol. 123, 1972).

McCready, H.W., 'The Cotton Famine in Lancashire in 1863' (HSLC *Transactions*, Vol. 106, 1954).

Milne, Graham J., 'Liverpool, Manchester and Market Power: The Ship Canal and the North Western business landscape in the late nineteenth century' (HSLC *Transactions*, Vol. 137, 2008).

Morgan, Philip, *Domesday Book Cheshire (including Lancashire)* (Phillimore Chichester, 1978).

Morrison, Michael B., *The Great English Golf Boom 1864–1914: A History* (Michael B. Morrison, 2022).

Orwell, George, *The Road to Wigan Pier* (Penguin 1986).

Padfield, H., *The Story of Ormskirk* (Carnegie Press, 1986).

Pevsner, Nikolaus, *Lancashire 1: the Industrial & Commercial South* (Yale University Press 2002)

Reidy, Michael S., 'Masters of Tidology, The cultivation of the physical sciences in early Victorian Liverpool' (HSLC *Transactions* Vol. 152, 2003).

Richmond L.A., 'Excavations on the Site of the Roman Fort at Lancaster 1950' (HSLC *Transactions*, Vol. 105, 1953).

Roberts, Alice, *The Celts: Search for a Civilisation* (Heron Books, 2015).

Roberts, Gordon, formby-footprints.co.uk (website, accessed 2024)

Roberts, Gordon, *The Lost World of Formby Point: Footprints on the Prehistoric Landscape, 5000 BC to 100 BC* (The Alt Press, 2014).

Roeder, C., 'Rise and Growth of Blackpool 1592–1792' (HSLC *Transactions*, Vol. 54, 1902).

Rose, Mary B., *Firms, Networks and Business Values: The British and American Cotton Industries since 1750* (Cambridge University Press, 2000).

Scarth, Alan, *Titanic and Liverpool* (National Museums Liverpool, 2009).

Sharples, Joseph, *The Oratory St James's Cemetery Liverpool* (National Museums & Galleries on Merseyside, 1991).

Smith, Stephen, Craig, 'Wigan's Mining and Mechanical School' (*Pastforward*, Wigan Council, 2021) .

Tonge, Mildred, 'The Lancashire Witches: 1612 and 1634' (HSLC *Transactions*, Vol. 83, 1931).

Unsworth, John, 'Cotton is King: Lancashire and the American Civil War' (*Pastforward*, Wigan Council, 2021).

Virgoe, John, 'Thomas Fleetwood and the Draining of Martin Mere' (HSLC *Transactions*, Vol. 152, 2003).

Wainwright F.C., 'The Anglian Settlement of Lancashire' (HSLC *Transactions*, Vol. 93, 1941).

Watson, M.I., 'William Billington: cotton operative, teacher and poet' (HSLC *Transactions*, Vol. 134, 1985).

White, Geoffrey H., 'The First House of Bellême', Transactions of the Royal Historical Society, Fourth Series, Vol. 22 (1940)

Wilson, C.F. Birkbeck, 'The records of a Liverpool "fireside", 1775–1781' (HSLC *Transactions*, Vol. 48, 1896).

Yorke, B. and R., *Britain's First Lifeboat Station, Formby, 1776–1918* (Alt Press, 2003).

INDEX

Abbey, Furness 15, 29, 43–4, 155
  Whalley 41, 44
Accrington Pals 167
Acts
  Combination 101
  Conventicle 66
  Employers Liability 95
  Equalities 160
  Factory 99
  Five Mile 66
  Law Breaking 102
  Mersey and Irwell 83
  Poor Law 113
  Reform 108, 127, 154
  Riot 101, 110, 111
  Slavery Abolition 137
  Ten Hours 104
  Truck 123
  Turnpike 89
Africa 78, 82, 136–8
agriculture 15, 17, 29, 39, 43–46, 48, 55, 70–2, 96, 109, 113, 120, 126, 133, 139
  hay 39, 70
  marl 11, 53, 72–3
  oats 29, 109–10, 113, 121, 150
  vaccaries 45–6
Ainsworth, Harrison 59
Aldred, Robert, Priest 71, 73
America 78, 80, 86, 97, 105, 127, 134, 136, 142, 150,
  civil war 128–30, 134, 141–2, 169
Anglican 66, 71, 138, 140, 168
Anti Corn Law League 120
architecture 44, 75, 166
  classical 75, 145–8
  Greek Revival 166
  Gothic 142, 145–8
Arkwright, Richard 99–101

Ashton under Lyne 87, 90, 127
Ashton, Lord 148
Astley 178
Atlantic 78, 128, 166
  Battle of 175–6
Barrow 120, 145, 148
Barrowford 88–9
Barton bridge 83–4, 165
Beaufort, Margaret 50
Bispham 73
Blackburn 60, 67, 85–6, 90, 100, 110, 119, 127–9, 133, 135, 142, 148–9, 169, 179–80, 181
Black Death 47–8
Blackpool 20, 73–4, 155–8, 160, 162, 171
Blackstone Edge 18–9
Blanketeers 105
Blundell (Crosby), Nicholas 71–2
  William the Cavalier 33, 63–5
  William the Recusant 32
Blundell family (Ince) 75
Bolton 55, 59, 61–2, 80, 90, 100, 114, 119, 127, 129, 132–3, 147, 169
Bootle 81, 148, 160, 175–6
Boteler, William 43
Boulder/Bowder Stone 11–2, 73
Bridgewater, Duke of 83–5, 94
Brigantes 16, 18, 21
Bright, John 170
Brindley, James 83
Bronze Age 15–6
Bulloch, Andrew Dunwoody 134
Burnley 75, 119, 142, 169, 179,
Burscough 44, 69,
Bury 59, 133, 149
canals 83–8, 114–5, 163–5, 172, 177

Bridgewater 83–6, 88, 94
Leeds & Liverpool 85–6, 88, 177
Sankey 88, 116
Caratacus 18
Cartimandua 18
Cartwright, Edmund 100
castles 17, 40–3, 57, 60, 158
  Clitheroe 41
  Lancaster 40, 57
  Motte and Bailey 41, 43
  Warrington 41, 43
Cathedral, Liverpool 139, 140, 168
  Manchester 56, 66
Catherwood, Mistress Mary, victualler 80
Catholic 32, 53, 59, 63, 65, 71, 139
Celts 15, 27
chapels 42, 44, 97, 136
  Clitheroe 41
  Crosby 71
    Cross Street, Manchester 67
    Didsbury 48
    Lady, Liverpool Cathedral 138, 140
  St Patrick's Heysham 34
  Turton 55
  Wigan workhouse 114
Charles I 58
Charles II 61, 62, 65–6
Charlie, Bonnie Prince 61, 63
Chartists 95, 121, 135
Chat Moss 115–6
Chatterton 111
Cheetham/Chetham, Humphrey 53–6
Chetham, George 55
  Library/School of Music 56, 152–3
China 128–9, 169–70
cholera 113, 138–9, 151
Chorley 90, 155
Christianity 24, 28, 34–5, 39
churches 39, 43–4, 114, 136, 138
  Christ Church, Accrington 167
  Halton on Lune 30
  Manchester, Parish and Collegiate 48, 55–6
  Ribchester 27
  Sefton, 71
  St Mary's, Lancaster (and Priory) 30
  St Mary's, Liverpool 80
  St Nicholas', Liverpool 87
  St Thomas', Liverpool 80
  St Oswald's, Winwick 30
  St Peter's, Formby 162
  St Peter's, Heysham 34
  Walton 39
  West Derby 39
  Whalley 31
Churchtown 70
Cistercian 43–4
Civil War 33, 50, 55–6, 59–63, 71
  American 128–30, 134, 141–2, 169
Clayton, Sarah 87–8
Clitheroe 41, 49, 124, 126–7, 129, 154
coal 11, 73, 77, 83, 85, 88, 90–9, 112, 114, 173–4, 177–180
  mine 73, 83–4, 92–4, 173, 178–9
Cobden, Richard 120, 155
Cockerell, Charles 147
colleges, see education
Colne 127, 129
Communist 152, 178
Co-operative 121–2, 130, 164
Corn Law 120, 149, 155
cotton 55, 57, 74–5, 85, 99–105, 109–11, 113–4, 122–136, 141–3, 148–52, 157, 159, 163, 168–172, 174, 177, 180
  exchange 142
  famine 112, 121
  Jenny 99, 100, 148
  loom 99–104, 110–1, 125, 130, 133, 169, 171
  mill 41, 75, 102–4, 109–11, 122–136, 139, 150, 155, 157, 159, 164, 171, 177, 179
  weaver 100–5, 110–1, 113, 121–36, 171
Crompton, Samuel 99–101, 149
Cropper, James 154

Index

Crosby 11–2, 32, 38, 63, 65, 71, 159
  Little Crosby 32
Cuerdale Hoard 31
Cunard 156, 166
Dane/Dane Law 29, 31
Darwell, Thomas 123
Darwen 129, 133, 170, 180
De Lacy family 41, 43
De Montgomery, Roger 37
De Poitou, Roger 37, 40
De Quincy, Thomas 151
Derby, (also Stanley), Lord, 3rd Earl of 50
  7th Earl of (also Strange) 59
  13th Earl of 101
  Charlotte, Countess of 61
Dickens, Charles 59, 152
Didsbury 48, 163
Dissenters 66–7,
Domesday Book 38–40, 48
Douglas, River 69
Eccleston, Thomas 70
education 44, 56, 66, 75, 100, 141, 179
  colleges 56, 76, 95
  libraries 31, 52, 56, 74, 95, 97, 121, 135, 139, 152–3
  schools 43–4, 53, 56, 58, 66–7, 94–5, 108, 113–4, 123–4, 129, 136, 138–41, 147, 151, 154, 177, 180
  universities 66, 138, 151, 178–9
Edward VII 127, 164
  the Confessor 40
  the Elder 31
Edwardian period 133
Egerton, Francis 83
Ellesmere, Countess of 94
Elmes, Harvey Lonsdale 145, 147
Engels 56, 152–3
Everton Football Club 165
Fairfax, Thomas 60–1
famine 47, 109, 112, 121, 139, 150
Fiennes, Celia 70
First World War 94, 158, 167, 169, 172

Fleetwood 69–70, 155–6
Fleetwood, Thomas 69–70
Formby 13–4, 76, 160–2
Forwood, Sir William 142
Foster, John Senior and Junior 75, 136
France 20, 37–8, 46, 50, 65, 78, 91, 100, 139
  Napoleonic War 75, 102, 107, 109, 113
Furness 15, 29, 43–4, 109, 155
Garnett, James 125, 128, 132
  Jeremiah 124–5
Gaskell, Elizabeth 150–2
Gaunt, John 48
Gawthorpe Hall 142
Gilbert, John 83
Gladstone family 137–8
golf 158–60
Grand Tour 75
Grey, Edward 154
Halls, Clayton 56
  Crosby 65, 71
  Crumpsall 54
  Free Trade 154
  Gawthorpe 142
  Hoghton 62
  Ince 124
  Motte and Bailey 42
  Rufford 69
  Speke 51–4
  St George's 140
  Standish 124
  Towneley 23–4
  (see also Town Hall)
Hargreave, James 99–100, 148
Harkirk Hoard 33
Harold I 39–40
Harold II 40
Harrison, Frederic 121, 140
Harwood, Betty 91
Haslingden 111, 122
Hawkshead 108
Hay, Revd W.R. 106, 108
Henry, Bishop 38
Henry I 38

Henry II 46
Henry IV (Bolingbroke) 48, 50
Henry VI 49
Henry VII (Tudor) 50
Henry VIII 50
Heysham Hogback 34–5
Hoghton, Richard 62
Hoghton Tower 62
Home Office 96, 123
Horrocks, William 100
Hulton, William 106
Hundred 39–40, 67
Hunt, Henry 105–6, 108
hunter-gatherers 12, 15
Huskisson, William 111, 115–8
Hussars 106, 108
Hyndman, Henry 150
Ice Age 13
Ireland 25, 29, 31–4, 46, 65–6, 85, 139
Iron Age 15
Isle of Man 29, 60–2, 73, 156
Jacobite 61–2, 72, 75, 78
James I 32, 62
James II 65–6
James III 62
John 46
Kay, John 99
Kersal Moor 95, 120, 159
Knowsley 50, 62
Kuerden, Dr 67
Lake District 11–2, 108
Lancaster 20, 30, 49, 58–9, 77–8, 86, 91, 96–7, 106, 110, 119, 139, 168
  Castle and Gaol 40, 37, 57–9, 106, 110
  Civil War 61–3
  Duke of 48–50
  Roman 20, 25, 37
  Town Hall 148, 168
Lathom 50, 60–2, 69
Leigh 59, 85, 113, 174, 178
Leyland 40
Liverpool, 52, 56, 77–81, 83–4, 86–8, 90–1, 128–9, 136–40, 142–3, 145–6, 154, 159, 161, 163, 166, 167–9, 176–9, 181
  Arena conference centre 165
  Black Death 46–8
  Cathedral 138, 140, 168
  Central Station 156
  Civil War 61, 63, 64
  Collegiate School 147
  Cunard Building 166
  docks 76–9, 136, 156, 165–6, 175
  Liver Building 166
  Liverpool & Manchester Railway 59, 91, 115–9, 149, 163
  Mersey Docks and Harbour Board Building 166
  Museum of Liverpool 165
  St George's Hall 140, 145–6,
  Three Graces 166
  Town Hall 145
  University 138
  Walker Art Gallery 75
Livesey, Joseph 112, 123, 134
London 49, 55, 58, 65–7, 77, 80, 83, 90, 94, 105, 111, 119, 121, 136, 149, 151–2, 154, 156, 165, 167, 170, 173, 180
Low Moor Mill 124, 128
Ludd/Luddite 102, 108
Lytham St Anne's 86, 160–2
Manchester 15, 19–20, 24, 45, 53, 55–7, 59, 74, 77, 83, 85–6, 90, 95, 104–5, 110, 118–9, 121–2, 126–7, 133, 135, 141, 147, 150–2, 154–5, 159, 167–8, 174, 178, 181
  Cathedral (Collegiate Church) 66
  Chamber of Commerce, 120, 170
  Chetham's Library 152
  Civil War 59–60, 65–7
  Corporation 163
  Free Library 56, 135
  Free Trade Hall 120
  Grammar School 53, 151
  Mechanics Institute 135
  National Football Museum 169
  Peterloo Massacre 105–6, 108

Pomona Botanical Gardens 164
Royal Exchange 143
Ship Canal 84–5, 163–5
Town Hall 146–7, 168
Martin Mere 45, 69–70
Marx, Karl 56, 152–3
Mersey, River 11, 19–20, 30, 37, 40–1, 46, 76, 79, 83–4, 134, 159, 181
Mexico Disaster 161
Middleton 102, 108
Morecambe 86, 156
Bay 15, 34, 43–4, 109, 148
Museums
British 23–4, 30–1, 75, 152
Burnley 75
Coal Mining 178
Lancaster 148
National Football 169
of Liverpool 165
of Victorian life 176
Preston 15
Ribchester 24
War 165
Wigan Pier 176–7, 181
Newcombe, Henry 66–7
Norris family 51
North Meols 77
Northumbria 30, 33
Nowell, Roger 57
Oldham 122, 133, 163, 169
Ormskirk 77
Pankhurst family 154
Parr Hall 87–8
Peel, Robert, father and son 101, 148–9
Pendle 24, 57–8
Pennines 11, 18, 28, 163
Penwortham 37, 40–1
Pen-y-Ghent 18
Piel Harbour 155
Pinder, Abraham 125–6
Poor Law 113
Poulton-le-Fylde 17, 155
Presbyterian 66

Preston 20, 44, 46, 49, 59, 74, 77, 86, 89–91, 97, 112, 119, 123, 129, 134–5, 169, 181
Civil War 59–63, 67
Dock 16
House of Correction 125
Mock Corporation 62
Moor 59
Museum 15
Town Hall 147
Protestant 65, 67
Puritan 63, 66, 96
Quaker 96–7, 120, 170
railways 86, 114, 120, 159, 180
Bolton &Leigh Railway 59
excursions 74, 155–6
Furness Railway 120
Grand Junction Railway 119
Lancashire & Yorkshire Railway 120, 168–9
Liverpool & Manchester Railway 59, 91, 115–9, 149, 163
manufacturers 168–9
Rainhill 116–7
Ramsbottom 140
Rathbone, Family 154
William 140
recusant 32, 64,
Restoration, the 55, 62, 65–6
Ribble, River 19–20, 23–4, 31, 37, 40–1, 63, 67, 70, 77, 127, 130, 160–1
Ribbleton Moor 61
Richard II 50
Richard III 50
riots 100, 110, 135, 137, 180–1
roads 27, 74, 77, 86, 96–7
motorways 20
Roman 19–20, 90
turnpikes 88–90
Robinson, Edmund (father and son) 58
Rochdale 66, 120–1, 135, 141, 147, 169
Roscoe, William 136, 154
Roses, War of 49

Rufford Old Hall 69
Runcorn 83–4, 86
Rupert, Prince 61–2
St Anne's 160–2
St Helens 87, 169, 174
Scarisbrick 69–70
schools, see Education
Scotland, Scots 43, 47–9, 52, 61–3
Second World War 159, 164, 167, 172, 175–6
Sefton 65, 71, 81
Shuttleworth, J.P. Kay 141–2
slaves, slavery 28, 39, 48, 77–8, 80–3, 87, 103–4, 123, 134, 136–8, 154
Southport 69, 119, 156, 160–2, 168, 172
Speke 38, 51, 53–4, 83
Stamford Bridge 40
Stanley Thomas, 50 (see also Derby)
Stephen, Count and King 43–4
Stephenson, George 59, 115–7
Stone Age
  Mesolithic 13
  Neolithic 13
  Palaeolithic 14
Strange, Lord (see Derby)
Stretford 164, 168
sugar 77–8, 83, 121, 138, 141
Thingwall 29
Titanic 165–6
Tory 134, 154
Town Hall, Accrington 147
  Barrow 148
    Bolton 147
  Bootle 148, 178
  Lancaster 148, 168
    Liverpool 145
  Manchester 145
  Preston 147
  Rochdale 147
Towneley Hall 23–4, 75

Townley family 75
trucking 122
turnpike 88–90
Turton Tower 55
Tyldesley, Thomas 73
Uhtred 38
Ulverston 15, 86, 109–10
Unitarian 67, 150
universities, see education
Upholland 91
vaccaries 45–6
Viking 29–34, 69
Walton, Liverpool 39, 48
Walton-le-Dale 20, 32, 67
Ward, John 125–6, 128–9, 131–2
Warrington 41, 43, 46, 61, 77, 83–84, 119, 135, 154, 164
Wellington, Duke of 107–8, 117, 149
West Derby 29, 39
Whalley 15, 24, 30–1, 41, 44, 58
Wigan 20, 61, 74, 91, 94–5, 113
  Pier 172, 176–7, 181
  Wiganspeak 91
Wilderspool 19–20, 46
Wilkinson, Kitty 138–9
William of Orange, and Mary 65
William the Conqueror 38, 40
Winwick 30, 61
witches 57–9
wool 46, 55, 85, 99
Wordsworth, William 108, 152
workhouses 67, 91, 112–4, 130, 150
Worsley 83, 85
Wyersdale 96–7

Yeomanry Cavalry 106
Yorkshire 16–7, 19, 26, 29, 43, 61